ALL ABOUT ENDANGERED SPECIES

Science & Research
STUDY GUIDE

By Laura Brown ~ Age 9
And Samara Booher ~ Age 12

The Thinking Tree, LLC
Copyright 2017
FunSchoolingBooks.com

TABLE OF CONTENTS

- 4 Sea Turtles
- 14 Snow Leopards
- 24 Red Pandas
- 34 Polar Bears
- 44 Miami Blue Butterflies
- 54 Manatees
- 64 Javan Rhino
- 74 Artic Foxes
- 84 Duck Billed Platypus
- 94 Whale Sharks
- 104 Honey Bees
- 114 Coral
- 124 South China Tiger
- 134 Axolotls
- 144 Southern Rockhopper Penguins
- 154 Golden Lion Tamarin
- 164 Savanna Elephants
- 174 Birds of Paradise
- 184 Okapis
- 194 Blue Whales
- 204 Iberian Lynxes
- 214 Pangolins
- 224 Western Lowland Gorillas
- 234 Black Footed Ferrets
- 244 Giant Pandas
- 254 Amur Leopards
- 264 Notes and Drawings

HOW TO USE THIS BOOK:

Follow the research prompts on each page. Use library books, the internet, documentaries, Wikipedia or any other parent approved research tools to discover more about each animal.

ALL ABOUT SEA TURTLES

WRITE DOWN FOUR FACTS ABOUT THIS KIND OF ANIMAL:

1. _____
_____

2. _____
_____

3. _____
_____

4. _____
_____

RESEARCH & DISCOVERIES
USE LIBRARY BOOKS, ENCYCLOPEDIAS OR THE INTERNET TO LEARN MORE.

SEA TURTLES

WRITE OR DRAW TO SHOW WHAT YOU LEARNED

LEARN & DRAW
SEA TURTLES

Draw My Habitat

Draw My Enemies

Draw My Food

Draw My Babies

WHY IS THIS ANIMAL ENDANGERED?

CREATE AN ILLUSTRATION TO SHOW THE PROBLEMS FACING THIS ANIMAL:

WHAT CAN BE DONE TO SOLVE THESE PROBLEMS?

WHERE IN THE WORLD DOES THIS ANIMAL LIVE?

Color the parts of the world where this animal lives.

WHAT OTHER ANIMALS LIVE IN THE SAME REGIONS?

_____   _____
_____   _____
_____   _____
_____   _____
_____   _____
_____   _____

STORY WRITING TIME

Look at the picture and write a story about it.

TITLE:

_____
_____
_____
_____
_____
_____
_____

WATCH A DOCUMENTARY ABOUT
SEA TURTLES

Draw a scene from your movie!

What did you learn?

DRAW A PICTURE OF THE ANIMAL

ALL ABOUT
SNOW LEOPARDS

WRITE DOWN FOUR FACTS ABOUT THIS KIND OF ANIMAL:

1. _____
_____

2. _____
_____

3. _____
_____

4. _____
_____

RESEARCH & DISCOVERIES
USE LIBRARY BOOKS, ENCYCLOPEDIAS OR THE INTERNET TO LEARN MORE.
SNOW LEOPARDS

WRITE OR DRAW TO SHOW WHAT YOU LEARNED

LEARN & DRAW
SNOW LEOPARDS

Draw My Habitat

Draw My Enemies

Draw My Food

Draw My Babies

WHY IS THIS ANIMAL ENDANGERED?

_____
_____
_____
_____
_____
_____
_____
_____
_____
_____

CREATE AN ILLUSTRATION TO SHOW THE PROBLEMS FACING THIS ANIMAL:

WHAT CAN BE DONE TO SOLVE THESE PROBLEMS?

_____
_____
_____
_____
_____
_____
_____

WHERE IN THE WORLD DOES THIS ANIMAL LIVE?

Color the parts of the world where this animal lives.

WHAT OTHER ANIMALS LIVE IN THE SAME REGIONS?

STORY WRITING TIME

Look at the picture and write a story about it.

TITLE:

_____

_____
_____
_____
_____
_____

WATCH A DOCUMENTARY ABOUT
SNOW LEOPARDS

Draw a scene from your movie!

What did you learn?

DRAW A PICTURE OF THE ANIMAL

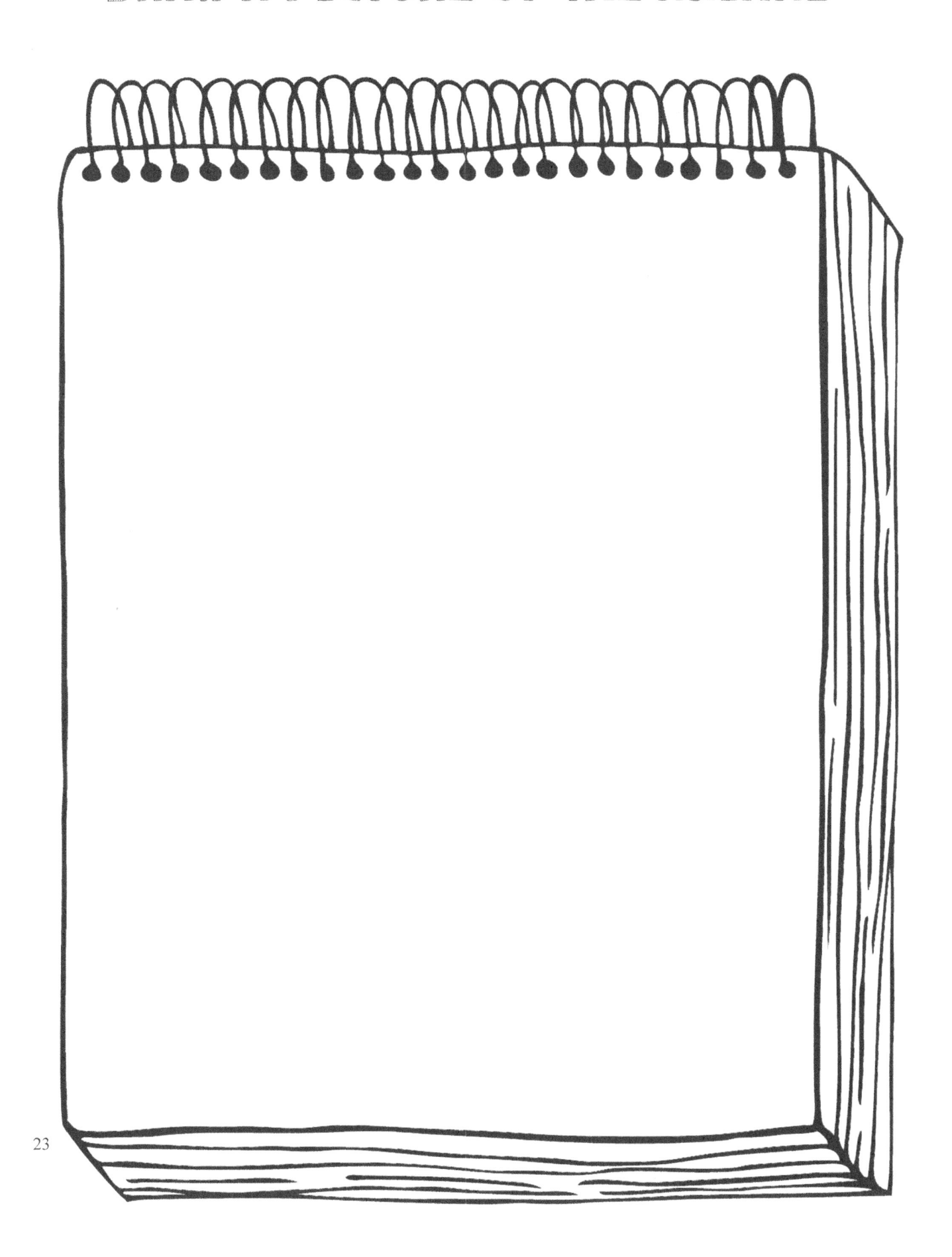

ALL ABOUT
RED PANDAS

WRITE DOWN FOUR FACTS ABOUT THIS KIND OF ANIMAL:

1. _____
_____

2. _____
_____

3. _____
_____

4. _____
_____

RESEARCH & DISCOVERIES
USE LIBRARY BOOKS, ENCYCLOPEDIAS OR THE INTERNET TO LEARN MORE.

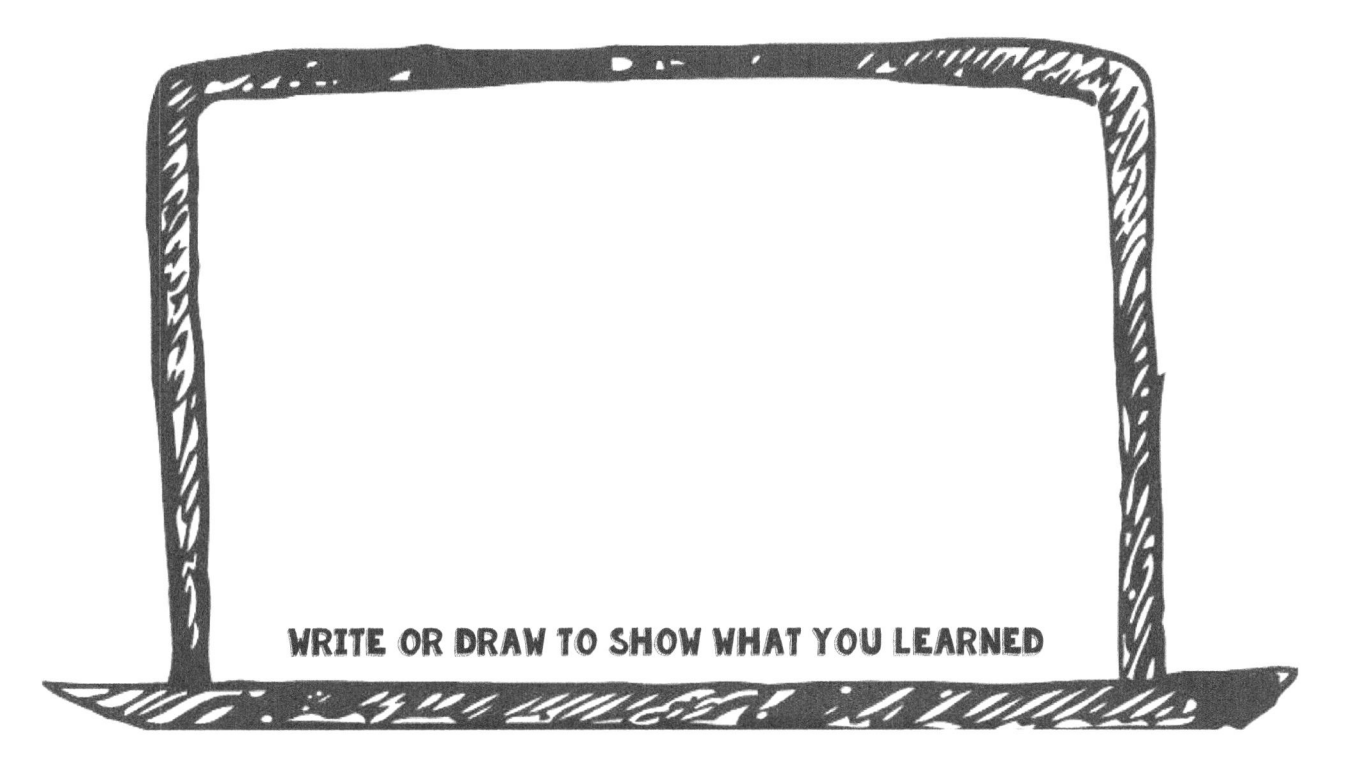

RED PANDAS

WRITE OR DRAW TO SHOW WHAT YOU LEARNED

LEARN & DRAW
RED PANDAS

Draw My Habitat

Draw My Enemies

Draw My Food

Draw My Babies

WHY IS THIS ANIMAL ENDANGERED?

_____
_____
_____
_____
_____
_____
_____
_____
_____
_____

CREATE AN ILLUSTRATION TO SHOW THE PROBLEMS FACING THIS ANIMAL:

WHAT CAN BE DONE TO SOLVE THESE PROBLEMS?

_____
_____
_____
_____
_____
_____
_____

WHERE IN THE WORLD DOES THIS ANIMAL LIVE?

Color the parts of the world where this animal lives.

WHAT OTHER ANIMALS LIVE IN THE SAME REGIONS?

STORY WRITING TIME
Look at the picture and write a story about it.

TITLE:

_____
_____
_____
_____
_____
_____
_____

WATCH A DOCUMENTARY ABOUT
RED PANDAS

Draw a scene from your movie!

What did you learn?

DRAW A PICTURE OF THE ANIMAL

ALL ABOUT
POLAR BEARS

WRITE DOWN FOUR FACTS ABOUT THIS KIND OF ANIMAL:

1. _____

2. _____

3. _____

4. _____

RESEARCH & DISCOVERIES
USE LIBRARY BOOKS, ENCYCLOPEDIAS OR THE INTERNET TO LEARN MORE.

POLAR BEARS

WRITE OR DRAW TO SHOW WHAT YOU LEARNED

LEARN & DRAW
POLAR BEARS

Draw My Habitat

Draw My Enemies

Draw My Food

Draw My Babies

WHY IS THIS ANIMAL ENDANGERED?

_____
_____
_____
_____
_____
_____
_____
_____
_____
_____

CREATE AN ILLUSTRATION TO SHOW THE PROBLEMS FACING THIS ANIMAL:

WHAT CAN BE DONE TO SOLVE THESE PROBLEMS?

_____
_____
_____
_____
_____
_____
_____

WHERE IN THE WORLD DOES THIS ANIMAL LIVE?

Color the parts of the world where this animal lives.

WHAT OTHER ANIMALS LIVE IN THE SAME REGIONS?

_____   _____
_____   _____
_____   _____
_____   _____
_____   _____
_____   _____
_____   _____

STORY WRITING TIME

Look at the picture and write a story about it.

TITLE:

WATCH A DOCUMENTARY ABOUT POLAR BEARS

Draw a scene from your movie!

What did you learn?

DRAW A PICTURE OF THE ANIMAL

ALL ABOUT
MIAMI BLUE BUTTERFLIES

WRITE DOWN FOUR FACTS ABOUT THIS KIND OF ANIMAL:

1. _____

2. _____

3. _____

4. _____

44

RESEARCH & DISCOVERIES
USE LIBRARY BOOKS, ENCYCLOPEDIAS OR THE INTERNET TO LEARN MORE.

MIAMI BLUE BUTTERFLIES

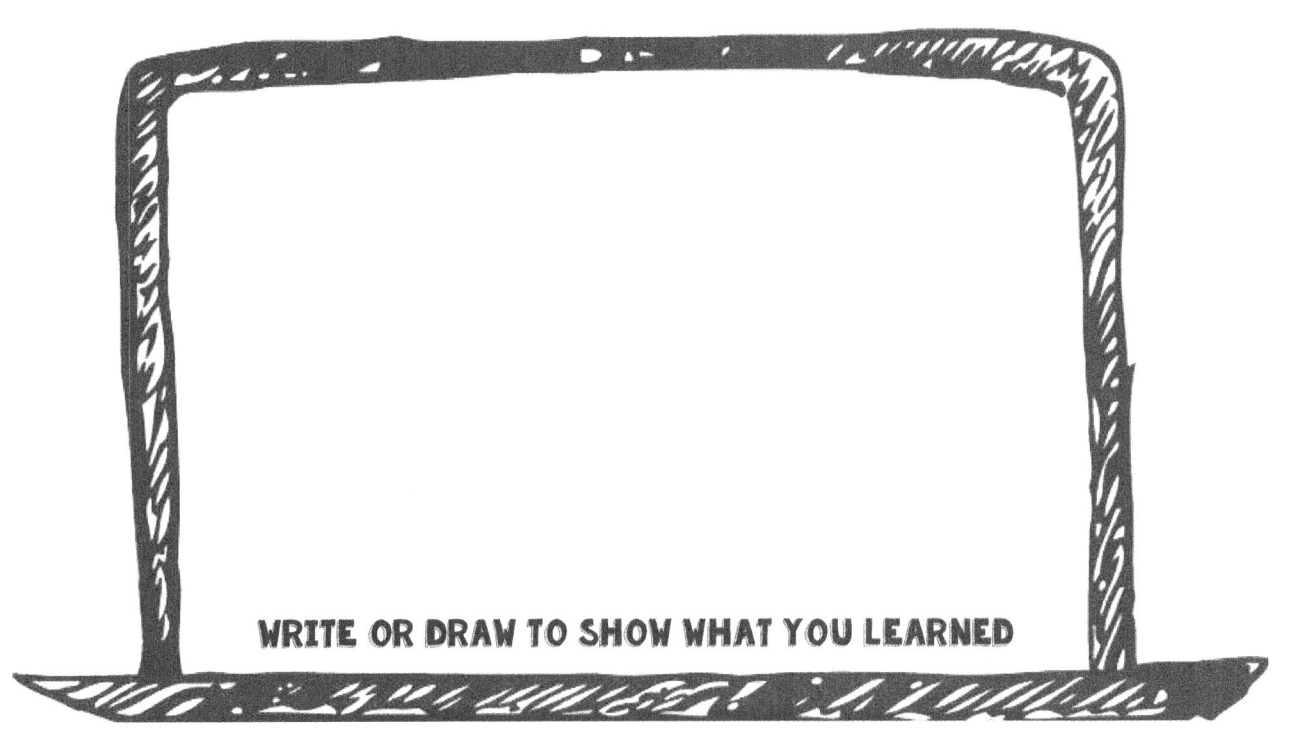

WRITE OR DRAW TO SHOW WHAT YOU LEARNED

LEARN & DRAW
MIAMI BLUE BUTTERFLIES

Draw My Habitat

Draw My Enemies

Draw My Food

Draw My Babies

WHY IS THIS ANIMAL ENDANGERED?

_____
_____
_____
_____
_____
_____
_____
_____
_____

CREATE AN ILLUSTRATION TO SHOW THE PROBLEMS FACING THIS ANIMAL:

WHAT CAN BE DONE TO SOLVE THESE PROBLEMS?

_____
_____
_____
_____
_____
_____

WHERE IN THE WORLD DOES THIS ANIMAL LIVE?

Color the parts of the world where this animal lives.

WHAT OTHER ANIMALS LIVE IN THE SAME REGIONS?

_____   _____
_____   _____
_____   _____
_____   _____
_____   _____
_____   _____

STORY WRITING TIME

Look at the picture and write a story about it.

TITLE:

_____

_____
_____
_____
_____
_____

WATCH A DOCUMENTARY ABOUT MIAMI BLUE BUTTERFLIES

Draw a scene from your movie!

What did you learn?

DRAW A PICTURE OF THE ANIMAL

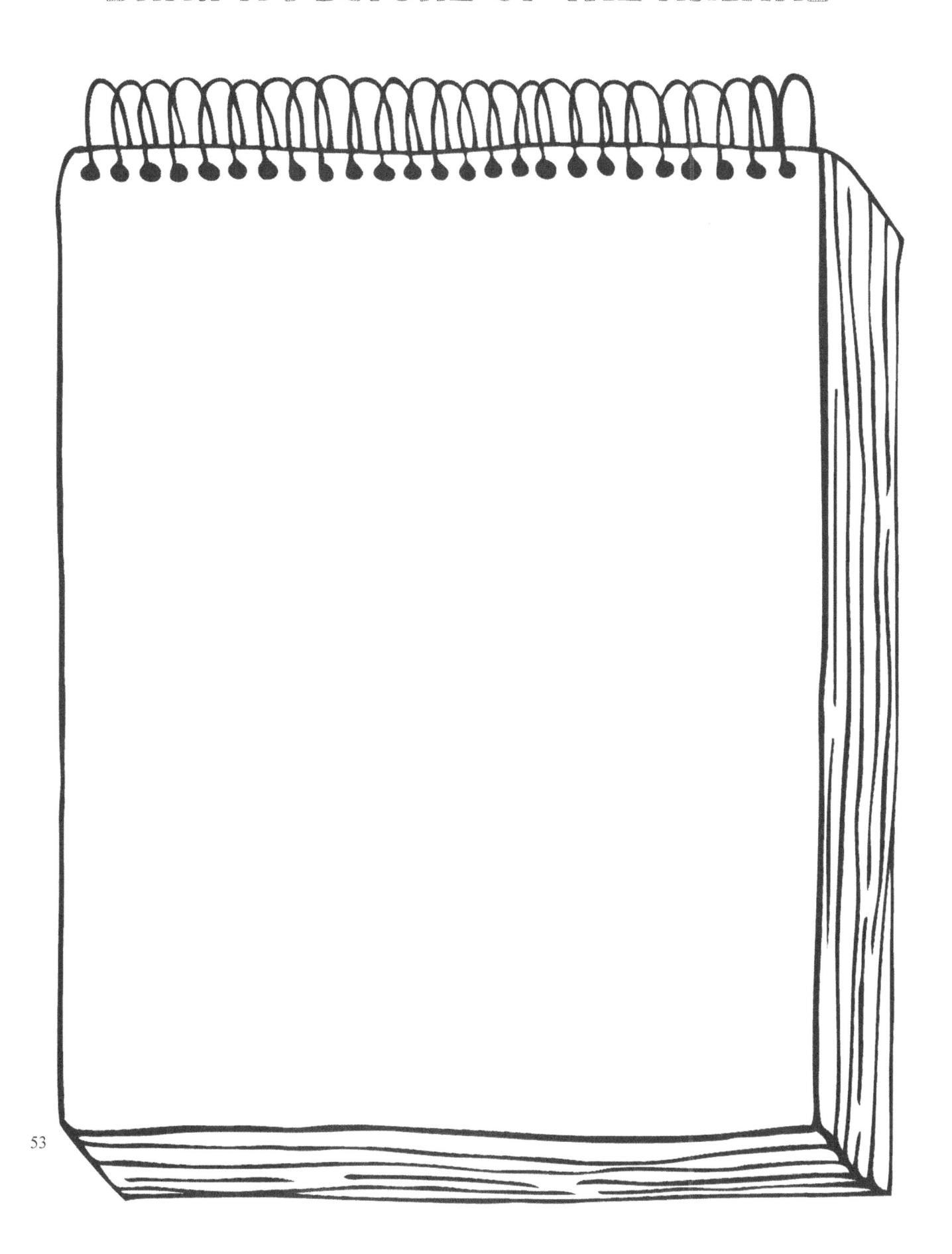

ALL ABOUT
MANATEES

WRITE DOWN FOUR FACTS ABOUT THIS KIND OF ANIMAL:

1. _____
   _____

2. _____
   _____

3. _____
   _____

4. _____
   _____

RESEARCH & DISCOVERIES
USE LIBRARY BOOKS, ENCYCLOPEDIAS OR THE INTERNET TO LEARN MORE.

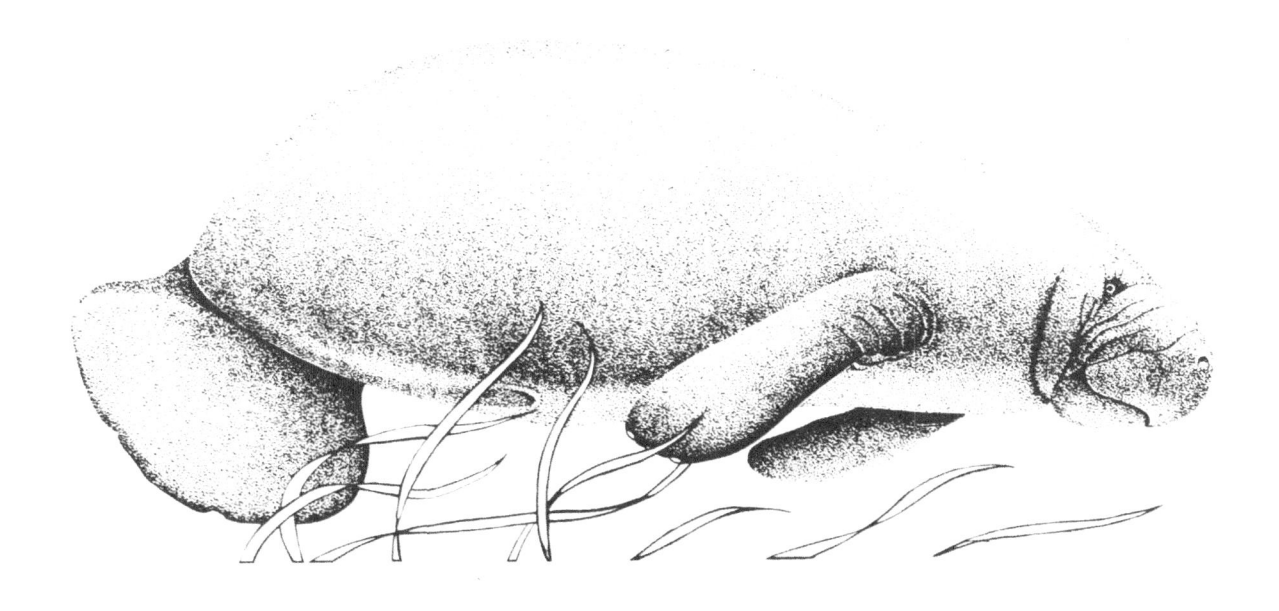

MANATEES

WRITE OR DRAW TO SHOW WHAT YOU LEARNED

LEARN & DRAW

MANATEES

Draw My Habitat

Draw My Enemies

Draw My Food

Draw My Babies

WHY IS THIS ANIMAL ENDANGERED?

_____
_____
_____
_____
_____
_____
_____
_____

CREATE AN ILLUSTRATION TO SHOW THE PROBLEMS FACING THIS ANIMAL:

WHAT CAN BE DONE TO SOLVE THESE PROBLEMS?

_____
_____
_____
_____
_____
_____

WHERE IN THE WORLD DOES THIS ANIMAL LIVE?

Color the parts of the world where this animal lives.

WHAT OTHER ANIMALS LIVE IN THE SAME REGIONS?

STORY WRITING TIME
Look at the picture and write a story about it.

TITLE:

_____
_____
_____
_____
_____
_____

WATCH A DOCUMENTARY ABOUT
MANATEES

Draw a scene from your movie!

What did you learn?

DRAW A PICTURE OF THE ANIMAL

ALL ABOUT JAVAN RHINOS

WRITE DOWN FOUR FACTS ABOUT THIS KIND OF ANIMAL:

1._____
_____

2._____
_____

3._____
_____

4._____
_____

RESEARCH & DISCOVERIES
USE LIBRARY BOOKS, ENCYCLOPEDIAS OR THE INTERNET TO LEARN MORE.

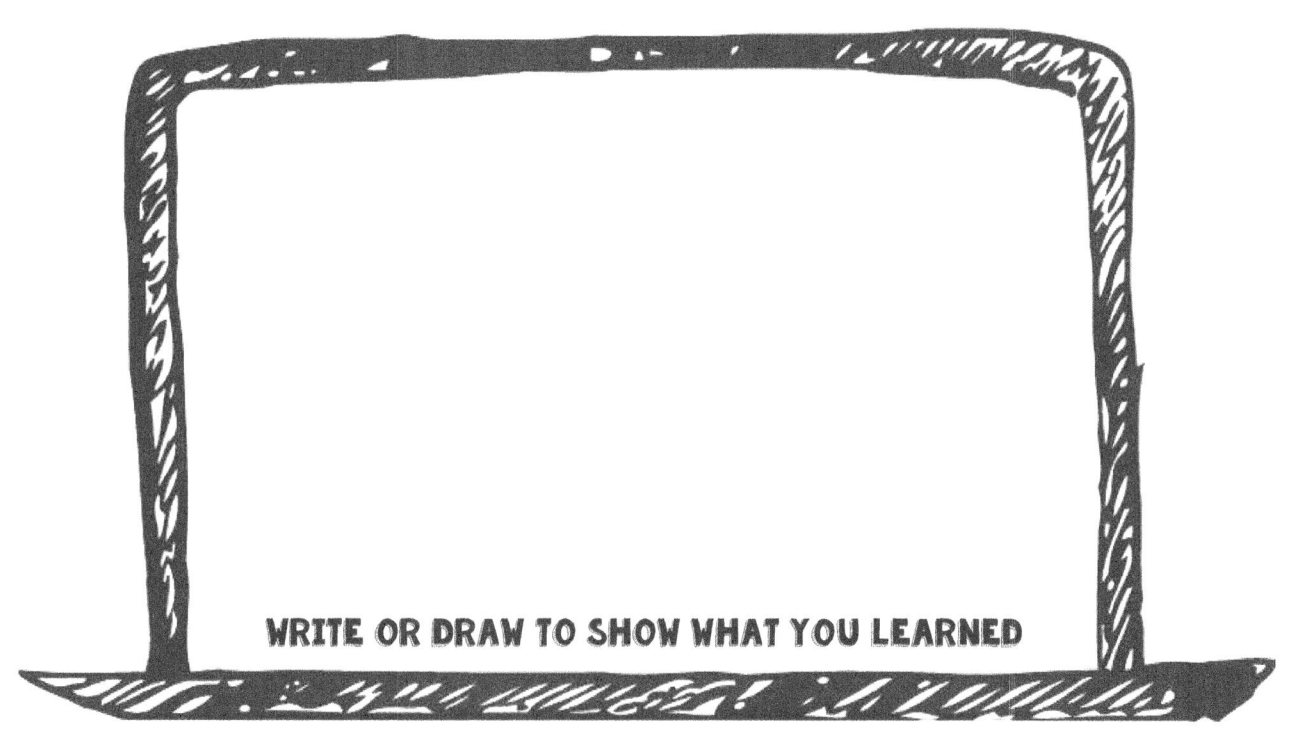

JAVAN RHINOS

WRITE OR DRAW TO SHOW WHAT YOU LEARNED

LEARN & DRAW
JAVAN RHINOS

Draw My Habitat

Draw My Enemies

Draw My Food

Draw My Babies

WHY IS THIS ANIMAL ENDANGERED?

_____
_____
_____
_____
_____
_____
_____
_____

CREATE AN ILLUSTRATION TO SHOW THE PROBLEMS FACING THIS ANIMAL:

WHAT CAN BE DONE TO SOLVE THESE PROBLEMS?

_____
_____
_____
_____
_____
_____

WHERE IN THE WORLD DOES THIS ANIMAL LIVE?

Color the parts of the world where this animal lives.

WHAT OTHER ANIMALS LIVE IN THE SAME REGIONS?

STORY WRITING TIME

Look at the picture and write a story about it.

TITLE:

_____
_____
_____
_____
_____
_____
_____

WATCH A DOCUMENTARY ABOUT JAVAN RHINOS

Draw a scene from your movie!

What did you learn?

72

DRAW A PICTURE OF THE ANIMAL

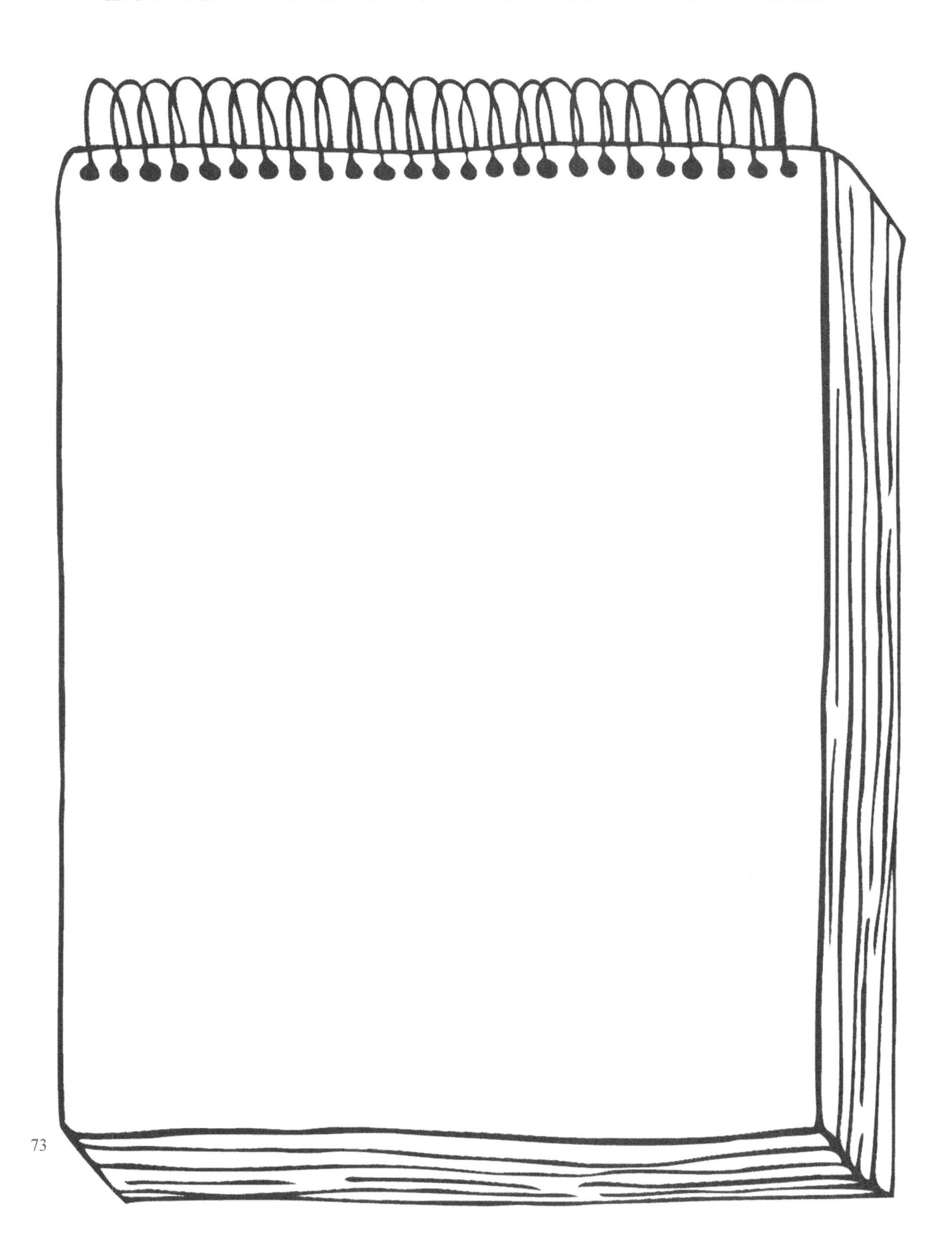

ALL ABOUT ARCTIC FOXES

WRITE DOWN FOUR FACTS ABOUT THIS KIND OF ANIMAL:

1. _____

2. _____

3. _____

4. _____

RESEARCH & DISCOVERIES
USE LIBRARY BOOKS, ENCYCLOPEDIAS OR THE INTERNET TO LEARN MORE.

ARCTIC FOXES

WRITE OR DRAW TO SHOW WHAT YOU LEARNED

LEARN & DRAW
ARCTIC FOXES

Draw My Habitat

Draw My Enemies

Draw My Food

Draw My Babies

WHY IS THIS ANIMAL ENDANGERED?

_____
_____
_____
_____
_____
_____
_____
_____
_____

CREATE AN ILLUSTRATION TO SHOW THE PROBLEMS FACING THIS ANIMAL:

WHAT CAN BE DONE TO SOLVE THESE PROBLEMS?

_____
_____
_____
_____
_____
_____

WHERE IN THE WORLD DOES THIS ANIMAL LIVE?

Color the parts of the world where this animal lives.

WHAT OTHER ANIMALS LIVE IN THE SAME REGIONS?

STORY WRITING TIME

Look at the picture and write a story about it.

TITLE:

_____

_____
_____
_____
_____
_____

WATCH A DOCUMENTARY ABOUT
ARCTIC FOXES

Draw a scene from your movie!

What did you learn?

DRAW A PICTURE OF THE ANIMAL

ALL ABOUT
DUCK BILLED PLATYPUS

WRITE DOWN FOUR FACTS ABOUT THIS KIND OF ANIMAL:

1. _____
_____

2. _____
_____

3. _____
_____

4. _____
_____

RESEARCH & DISCOVERIES
USE LIBRARY BOOKS, ENCYCLOPEDIAS OR THE INTERNET TO LEARN MORE.

DUCK BILLED PLATYPUS

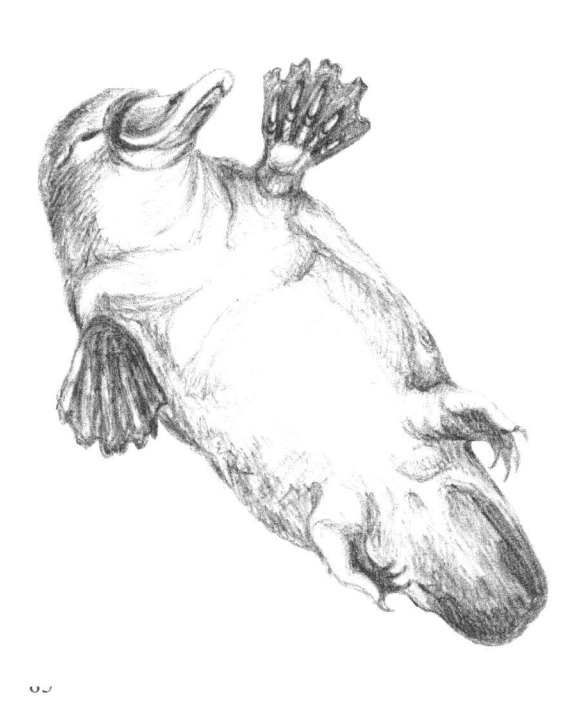

WRITE OR DRAW TO SHOW WHAT YOU LEARNED

LEARN & DRAW
DUCK BILLED PLATYPUS

Draw My Habitat

Draw My Enemies

Draw My Food

Draw My Babies

WHY IS THIS ANIMAL ENDANGERED?

_____
_____
_____
_____
_____
_____
_____
_____

CREATE AN ILLUSTRATION TO SHOW THE PROBLEMS FACING THIS ANIMAL:

WHAT CAN BE DONE TO SOLVE THESE PROBLEMS?

_____
_____
_____
_____
_____
_____

WHERE IN THE WORLD DOES THIS ANIMAL LIVE?

Color the parts of the world where this animal lives.

WHAT OTHER ANIMALS LIVE IN THE SAME REGIONS?

STORY WRITING TIME
Look at the picture and write a story about it.

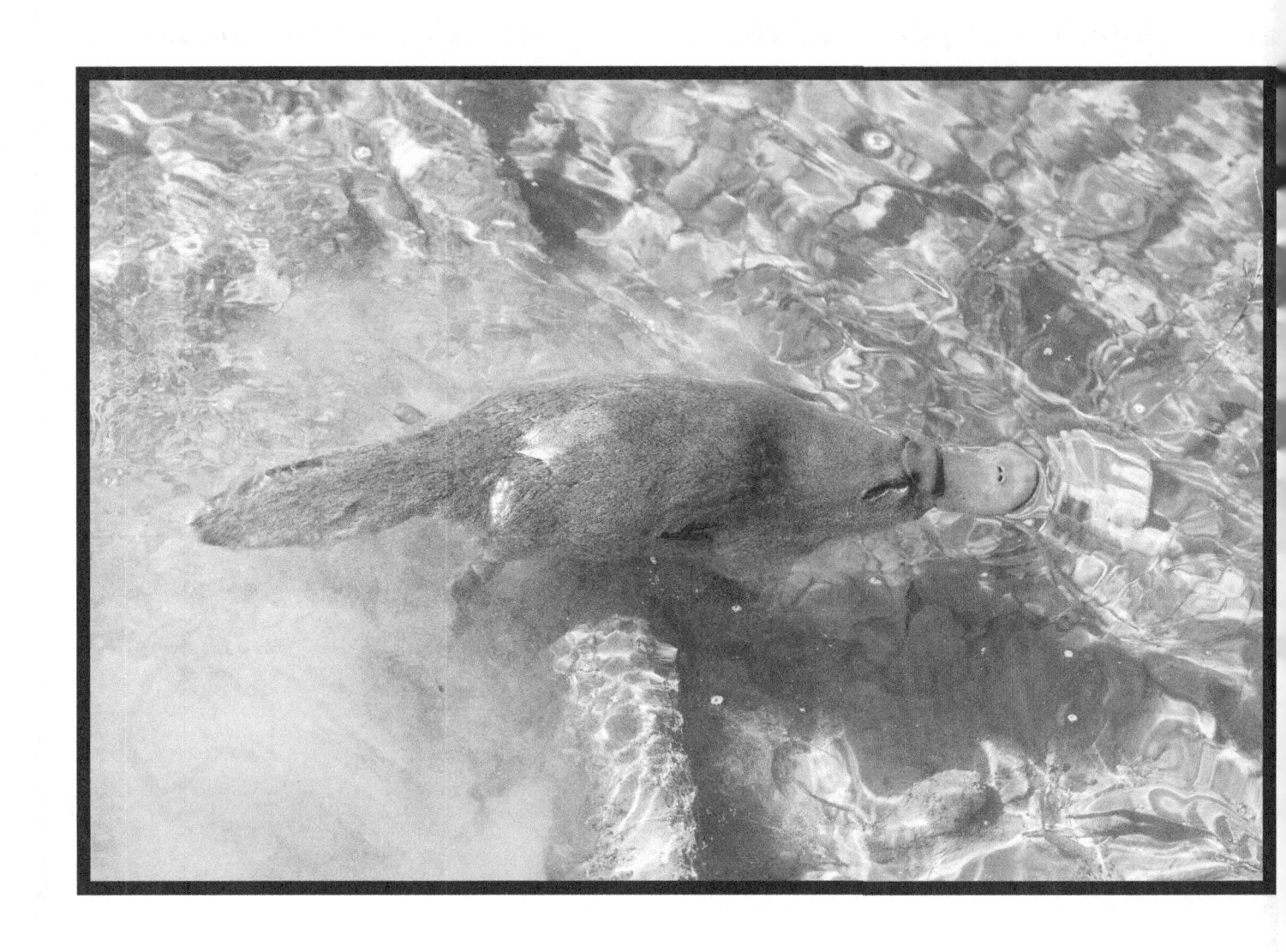

TITLE:

WATCH A DOCUMENTARY ABOUT DUCK BILLED PLATYPUS

Draw a scene from your movie!

What did you learn?

DRAW A PICTURE OF THE ANIMAL

ALL ABOUT WHALE SHARKS

WRITE DOWN FOUR FACTS ABOUT THIS KIND OF ANIMAL:

1. _____

2. _____

3. _____

4. _____

RESEARCH & DISCOVERIES
USE LIBRARY BOOKS, ENCYCLOPEDIAS OR THE INTERNET TO LEARN MORE.

WHALE SHARKS

WRITE OR DRAW TO SHOW WHAT YOU LEARNED

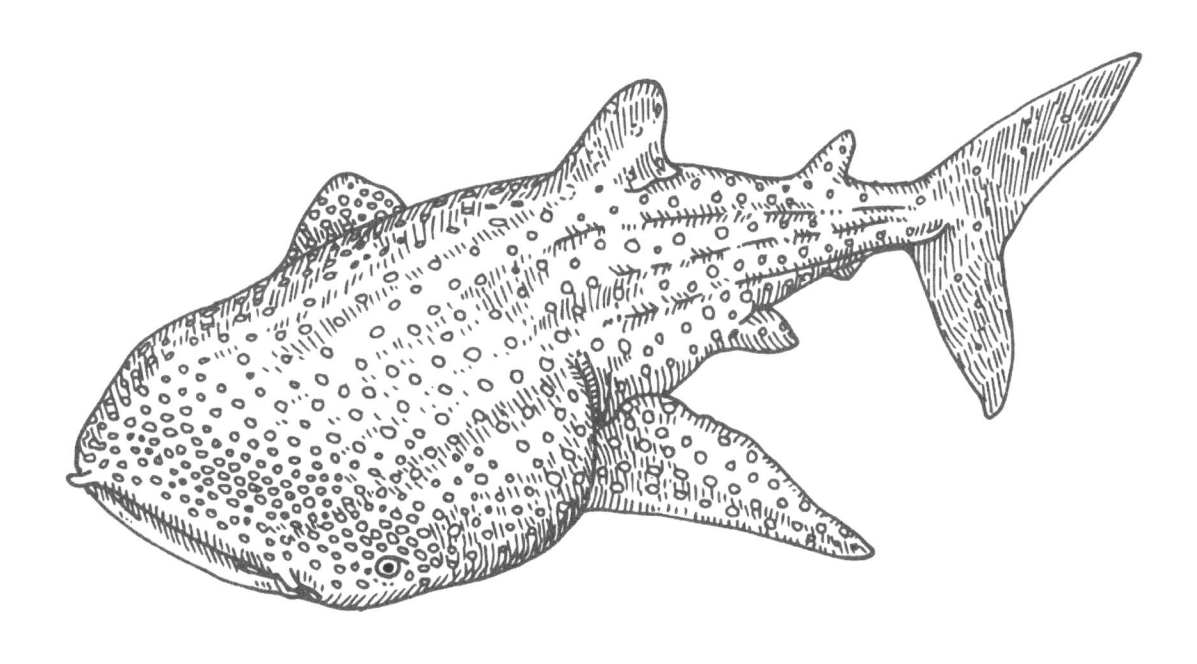

LEARN & DRAW
WHALE SHARKS

Draw My Habitat

Draw My Enemies

Draw My Food

Draw My Babies

WHY IS THIS ANIMAL ENDANGERED?

_____
_____
_____
_____
_____
_____
_____
_____

CREATE AN ILLUSTRATION TO SHOW THE PROBLEMS FACING THIS ANIMAL:

WHAT CAN BE DONE TO SOLVE THESE PROBLEMS?

_____
_____
_____
_____
_____
_____

WHERE IN THE WORLD DOES THIS ANIMAL LIVE?

Color the parts of the world where this animal lives.

WHAT OTHER ANIMALS LIVE IN THE SAME REGIONS?

STORY WRITING TIME

Look at the picture and write a story about it.

TITLE:

WATCH A DOCUMENTARY ABOUT
WHALE SHARK

Draw a scene from your movie!

What did you learn?

DRAW A PICTURE OF THE ANIMAL

ALL ABOUT HONEY BEES

WRITE DOWN FOUR FACTS ABOUT THIS KIND OF ANIMAL:

1. _____

2. _____

3. _____

4. _____

RESEARCH & DISCOVERIES
USE LIBRARY BOOKS, ENCYCLOPEDIAS OR THE INTERNET TO LEARN MORE.

HONEY BEES

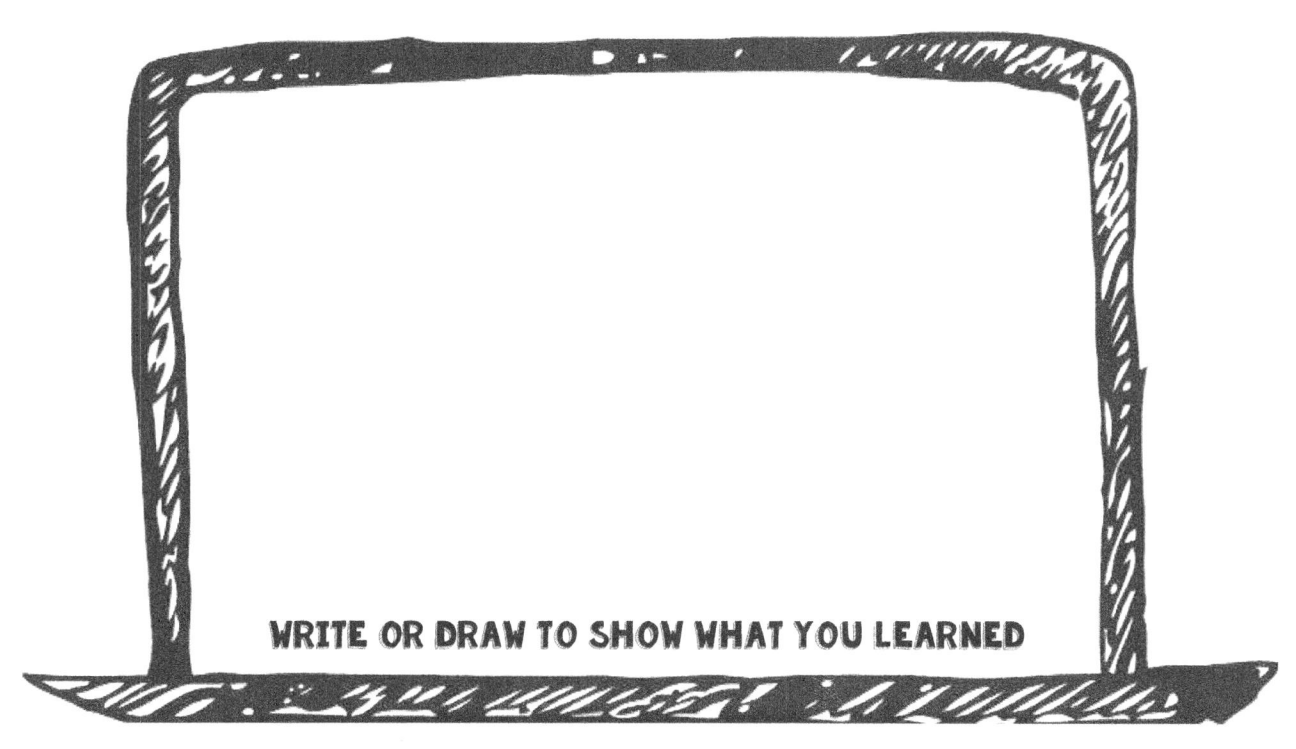

WRITE OR DRAW TO SHOW WHAT YOU LEARNED

LEARN & DRAW
HONEY BEES

Draw My Habitat

Draw My Enemies

Draw My Food

Draw My Babies

WHY IS THIS ANIMAL ENDANGERED?

_____
_____
_____
_____
_____
_____
_____
_____
_____
_____

CREATE AN ILLUSTRATION TO SHOW THE PROBLEMS FACING THIS ANIMAL:

WHAT CAN BE DONE TO SOLVE THESE PROBLEMS?

_____
_____
_____
_____
_____
_____

WHERE IN THE WORLD DOES THIS ANIMAL LIVE?

Color the parts of the world where this animal lives.

WHAT OTHER ANIMALS LIVE IN THE SAME REGIONS?

STORY WRITING TIME

Look at the picture and write a story about it.

TITLE:

_____
_____
_____
_____
_____
_____

WATCH A DOCUMENTARY ABOUT HONEY BEES

Draw a scene from your movie!

What did you learn?

DRAW A PICTURE OF THE ANIMAL

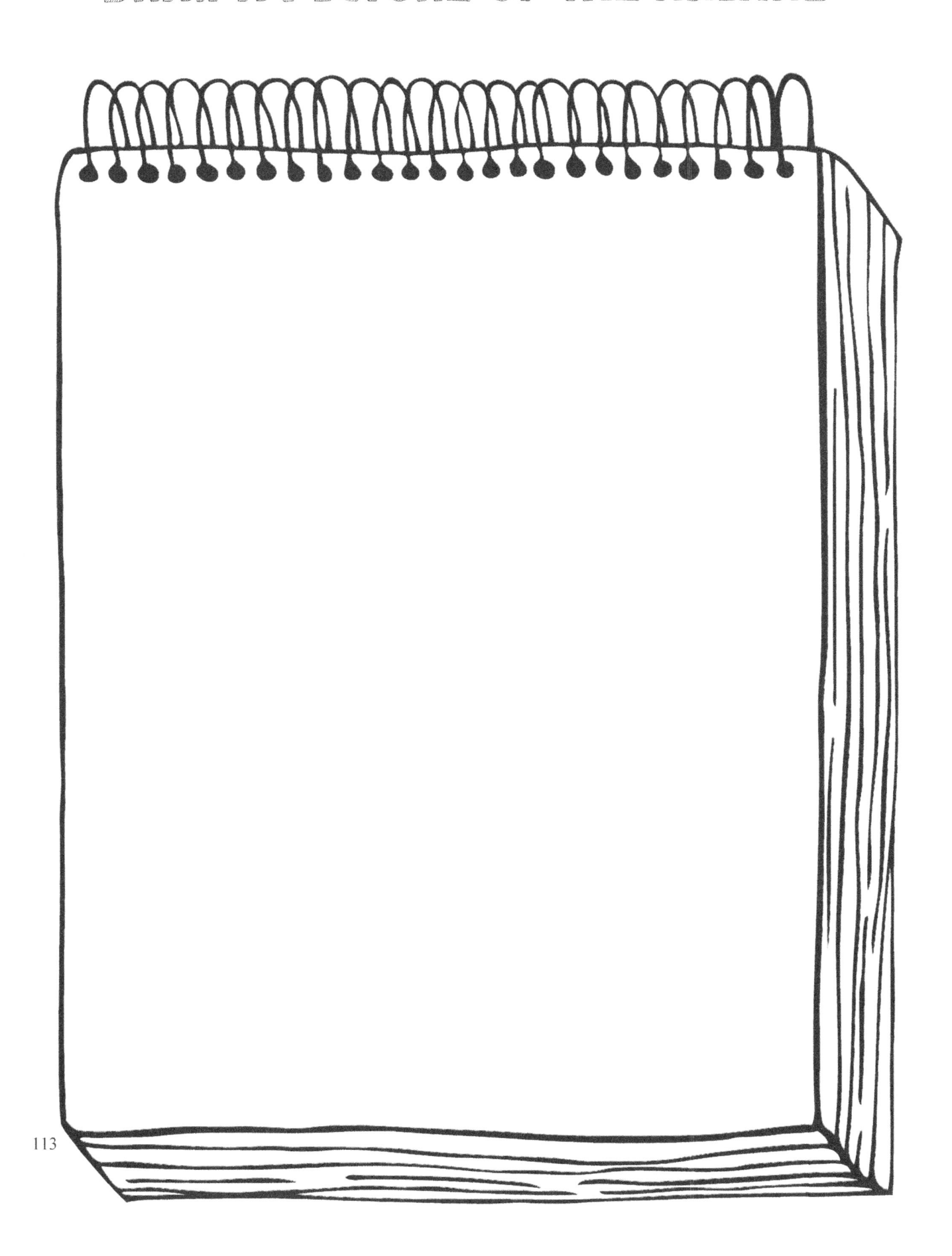

ALL ABOUT
CORAL

WRITE DOWN FOUR FACTS ABOUT THIS KIND OF ANIMAL:

1. _____

2. _____

3. _____

4. _____

RESEARCH & DISCOVERIES
USE LIBRARY BOOKS, ENCYCLOPEDIAS OR THE INTERNET TO LEARN MORE.
CORAL

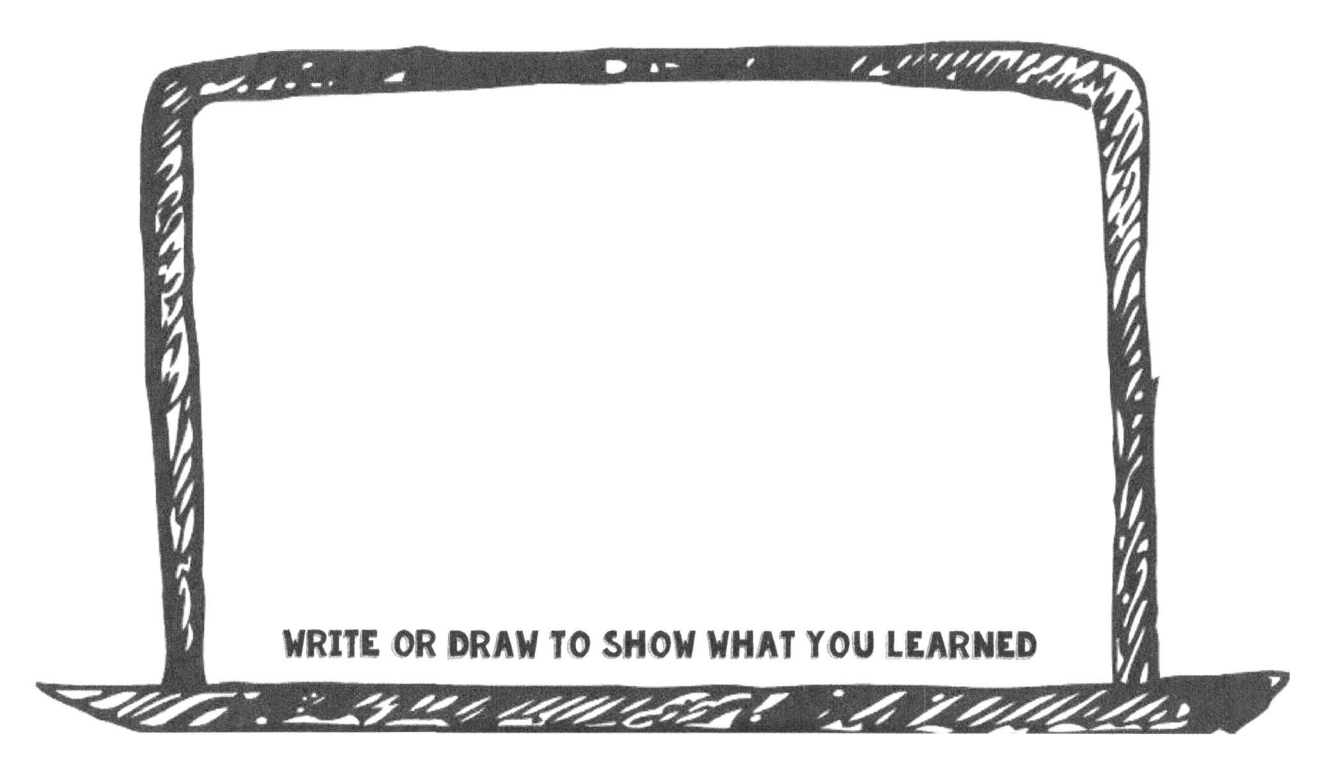

WRITE OR DRAW TO SHOW WHAT YOU LEARNED

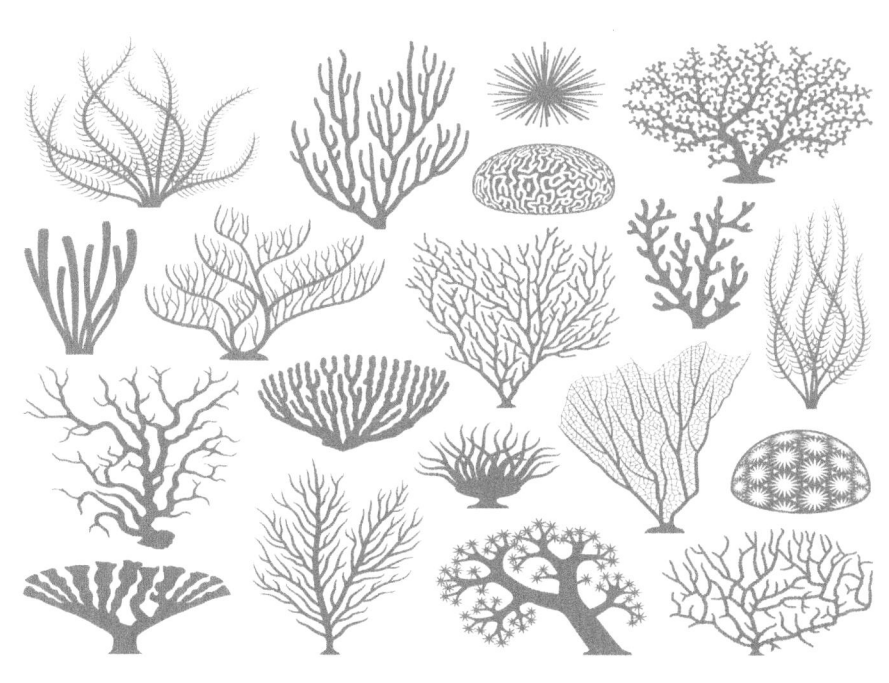

LEARN & DRAW
CORAL

Draw My Habitat

Draw My Enemies

Draw My Food

Draw My Babies

WHY IS THIS ANIMAL ENDANGERED?

CREATE AN ILLUSTRATION TO SHOW THE PROBLEMS FACING THIS ANIMAL:

WHAT CAN BE DONE TO SOLVE THESE PROBLEMS?

WHERE IN THE WORLD DOES THIS ANIMAL LIVE?

Color the parts of the world where this animal lives.

WHAT OTHER ANIMALS LIVE IN THE SAME REGIONS?

119

STORY WRITING TIME

Look at the picture and write a story about it.

TITLE:

_____
_____
_____
_____
_____
_____
_____

WATCH A DOCUMENTARY ABOUT
CORAL

Draw a scene from your movie!

What did you learn?

DRAW A PICTURE OF THE ANIMAL

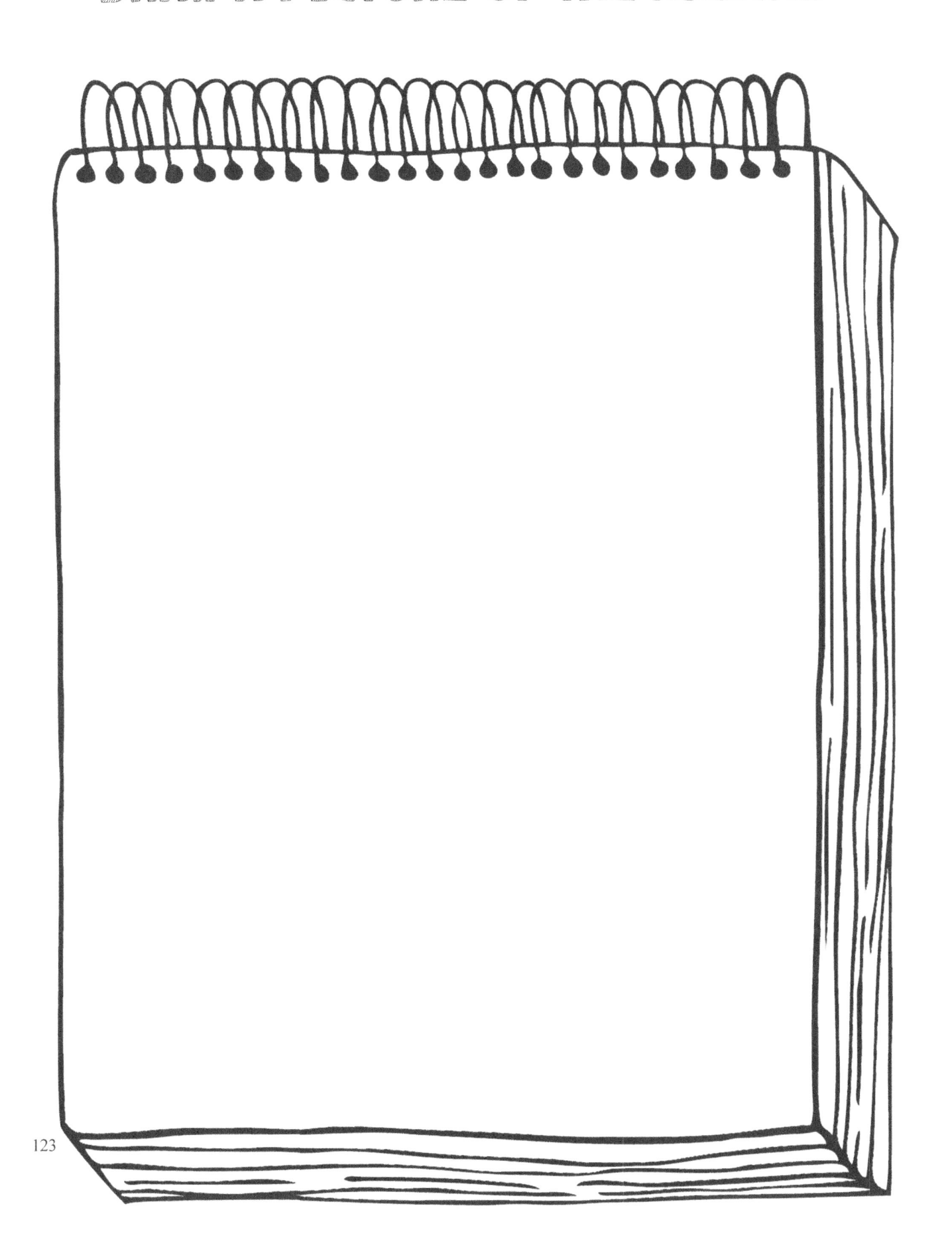

ALL ABOUT SOUTH CHINA TIGERS

WRITE DOWN FOUR FACTS ABOUT THIS KIND OF ANIMAL:

1. _____

2. _____

3. _____

4. _____

RESEARCH & DISCOVERIES
USE LIBRARY BOOKS, ENCYCLOPEDIAS OR THE INTERNET TO LEARN MORE.

SOUTH CHINA TIGERS

WRITE OR DRAW TO SHOW WHAT YOU LEARNED

LEARN & DRAW
SOUTH CHINA TIGERS

Draw My Habitat

Draw My Enemies

Draw My Food

Draw My Babies

WHY IS THIS ANIMAL ENDANGERED?

_____
_____
_____
_____
_____
_____
_____
_____
_____

CREATE AN ILLUSTRATION TO SHOW THE PROBLEMS FACING THIS ANIMAL:

WHAT CAN BE DONE TO SOLVE THESE PROBLEMS?

_____
_____
_____
_____
_____
_____

WHERE IN THE WORLD DOES THIS ANIMAL LIVE?

Color the parts of the world where this animal lives.

WHAT OTHER ANIMALS LIVE IN THE SAME REGIONS?

STORY WRITING TIME
Look at the picture and write a story about it.

TITLE:

WATCH A DOCUMENTARY ABOUT SOUTH CHINA TIGERS

Draw a scene from your movie!

What did you learn?

DRAW A PICTURE OF THE ANIMAL

ALL ABOUT
AXOLOTLS

WRITE DOWN FOUR FACTS ABOUT THIS KIND OF ANIMAL:

1. _____
_____

2. _____
_____

3. _____
_____

4. _____
_____

RESEARCH & DISCOVERIES
USE LIBRARY BOOKS, ENCYCLOPEDIAS OR THE INTERNET TO LEARN MORE.

AXOLOTLS

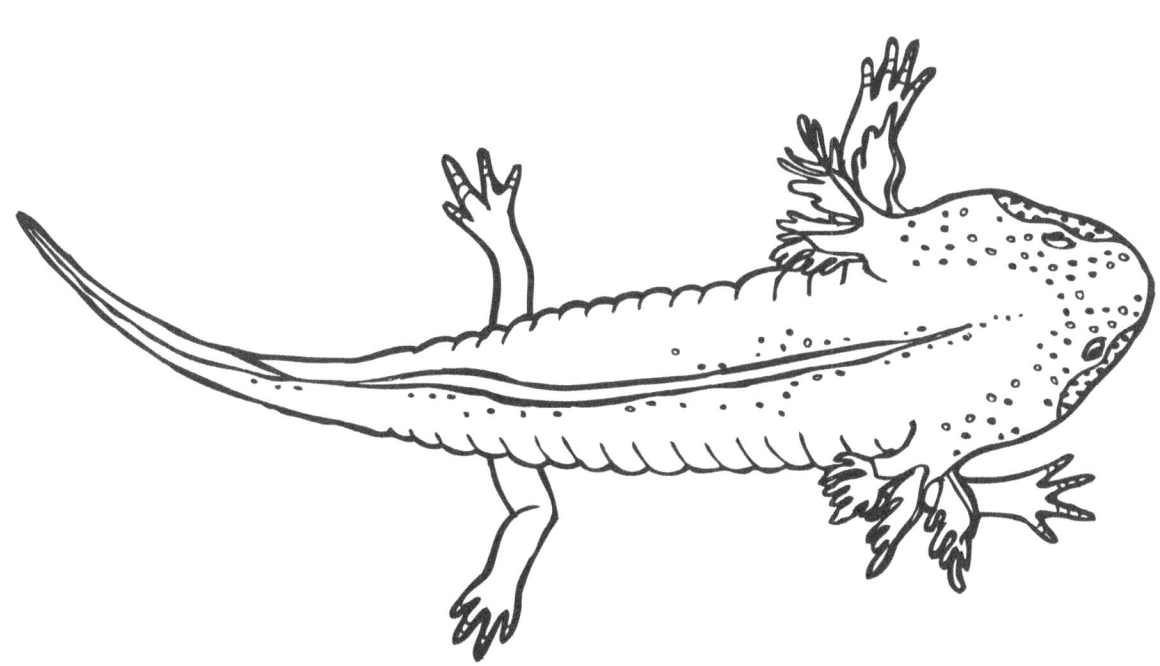

WRITE OR DRAW TO SHOW WHAT YOU LEARNED

LEARN & DRAW

AXOLOTLS

Draw My Habitat

Draw My Enemies

Draw My Food

Draw My Babies

WHY IS THIS ANIMAL ENDANGERED?

_____
_____
_____
_____
_____
_____
_____
_____
_____

CREATE AN ILLUSTRATION TO SHOW THE PROBLEMS FACING THIS ANIMAL:

WHAT CAN BE DONE TO SOLVE THESE PROBLEMS?

_____
_____
_____
_____
_____
_____

WHERE IN THE WORLD DOES THIS ANIMAL LIVE?

Color the parts of the world where this animal lives.

WHAT OTHER ANIMALS LIVE IN THE SAME REGIONS?

_____   _____
_____   _____
_____   _____
_____   _____
_____   _____
_____   _____

STORY WRITING TIME

Look at the picture and write a story about it.

TITLE: _____

_____
_____
_____
_____
_____
_____

WATCH A DOCUMENTARY ABOUT
AXOLOTLS

Draw a scene from your movie!

What did you learn?

DRAW A PICTURE OF THE ANIMAL

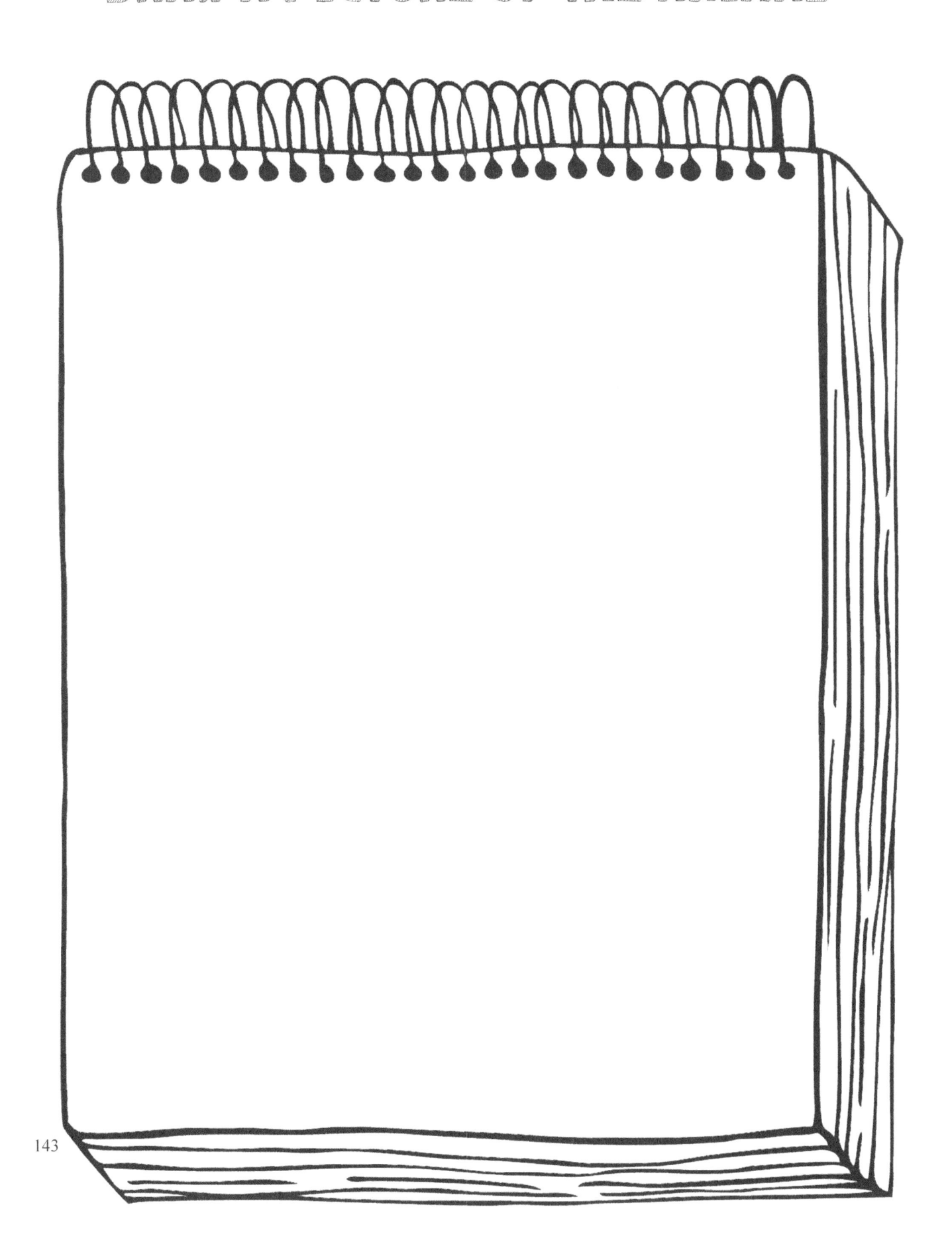

ALL ABOUT SOUTHERN ROCKHOPPER PENGUINS

WRITE DOWN FOUR FACTS ABOUT THIS KIND OF ANIMAL:

1. _____

2. _____

3. _____

4. _____

RESEARCH & DISCOVERIES
USE LIBRARY BOOKS, ENCYCLOPEDIAS OR THE INTERNET TO LEARN MORE.

SOUTHERN ROCKHOPPER PENGUINS

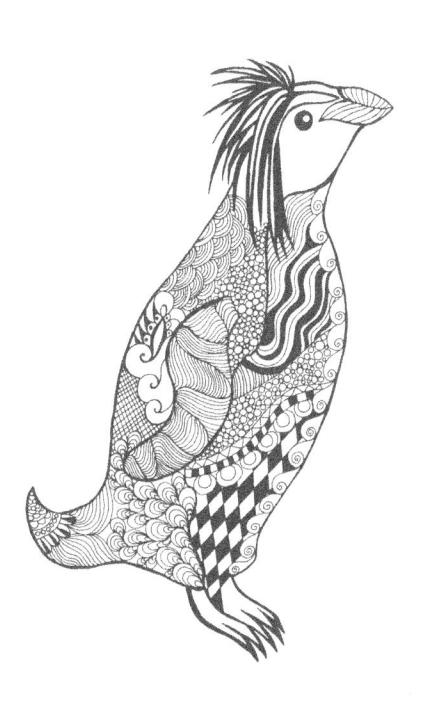

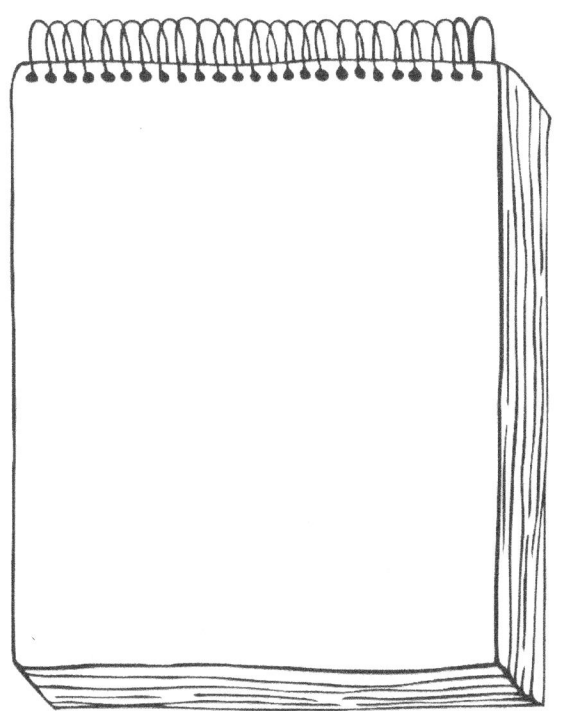

WRITE OR DRAW TO SHOW WHAT YOU LEARNED

145

LEARN & DRAW

SOUTHERN ROCKHOPPER PENGUINS

Draw My Habitat

Draw My Enemies

Draw My Food

Draw My Babies

WHY IS THIS ANIMAL ENDANGERED?

_____
_____
_____
_____
_____
_____
_____
_____
_____

CREATE AN ILLUSTRATION TO SHOW THE PROBLEMS FACING THIS ANIMAL:

WHAT CAN BE DONE TO SOLVE THESE PROBLEMS?

_____
_____
_____
_____
_____
_____

WHERE IN THE WORLD DOES THIS ANIMAL LIVE?

Color the parts of the world where this animal lives.

WHAT OTHER ANIMALS LIVE IN THE SAME REGIONS?

STORY WRITING TIME
Look at the picture and write a story about it.

TITLE:

_____
_____
_____
_____
_____
_____

WATCH A DOCUMENTARY ABOUT SOUTHERN ROCKHOPPER PENGUINS

Draw a scene from your movie!

What did you learn?

DRAW A PICTURE OF THE ANIMAL

ALL ABOUT
GOLDEN LION TAMARINS

WRITE DOWN FOUR FACTS ABOUT THIS KIND OF ANIMAL:

1. _____

2. _____

3. _____

4. _____

RESEARCH & DISCOVERIES
USE LIBRARY BOOKS, ENCYCLOPEDIAS OR THE INTERNET TO LEARN MORE.

GOLDEN LION TAMARINS

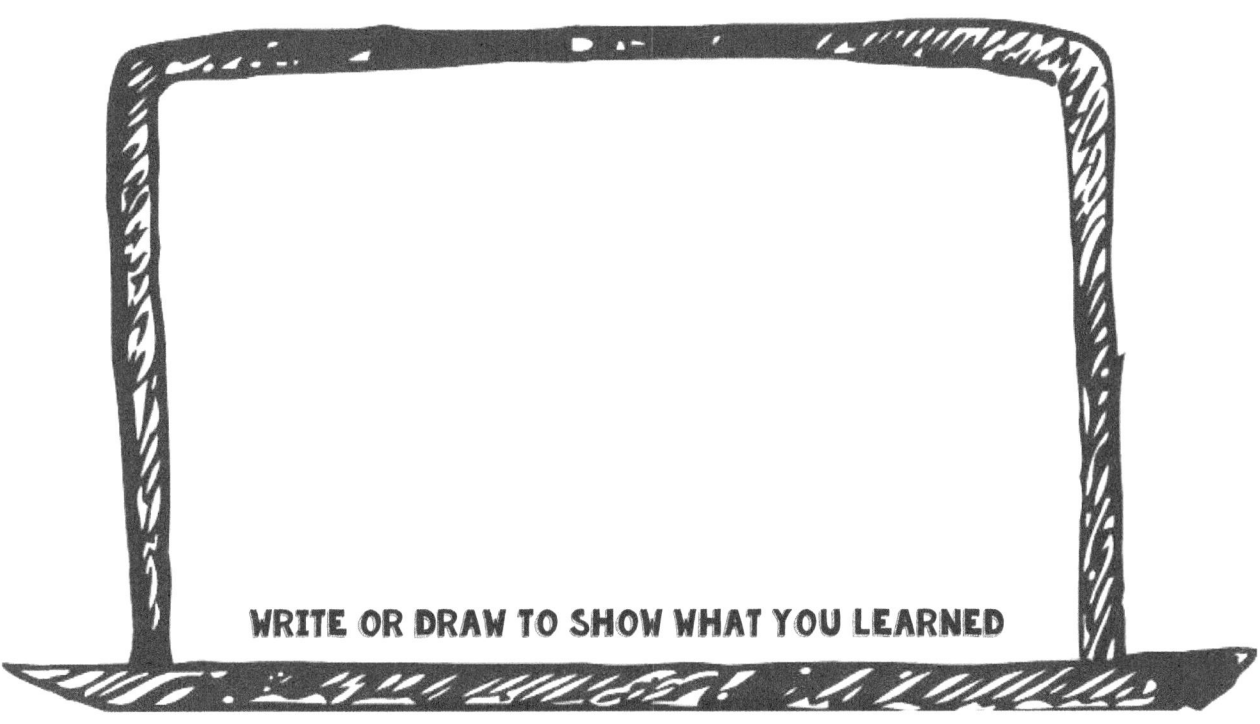

WRITE OR DRAW TO SHOW WHAT YOU LEARNED

LEARN & DRAW
GOLDEN LION TAMARINS

Draw My Habitat

Draw My Enemies

Draw My Food

Draw My Babies

WHY IS THIS ANIMAL ENDANGERED?

CREATE AN ILLUSTRATION TO SHOW THE PROBLEMS FACING THIS ANIMAL:

WHAT CAN BE DONE TO SOLVE THESE PROBLEMS?

WHERE IN THE WORLD DOES THIS ANIMAL LIVE?

Color the parts of the world where this animal lives.

WHAT OTHER ANIMALS LIVE IN THE SAME REGIONS?

159

STORY WRITING TIME

Look at the picture and write a story about it.

TITLE:

WATCH A DOCUMENTARY ABOUT GOLDEN LION TAMARINS

Draw a scene from your movie!

What did you learn?

DRAW A PICTURE OF THE ANIMAL

ALL ABOUT
SAVANNA ELEPHANTS

WRITE DOWN FOUR FACTS ABOUT THIS KIND OF ANIMAL:

1. _____
_____

2. _____
_____

3. _____
_____

4. _____
_____

RESEARCH & DISCOVERIES
USE LIBRARY BOOKS, ENCYCLOPEDIAS OR THE INTERNET TO LEARN MORE.

SAVANNA ELEPHANTS

WRITE OR DRAW TO SHOW WHAT YOU LEARNED

LEARN & DRAW
SAVANNA ELEPHANTS

Draw My Habitat

Draw My Enemies

Draw My Food

Draw My Babies

WHY IS THIS ANIMAL ENDANGERED?

_____
_____
_____
_____
_____
_____
_____
_____
_____

CREATE AN ILLUSTRATION TO SHOW THE PROBLEMS FACING THIS ANIMAL:

WHAT CAN BE DONE TO SOLVE THESE PROBLEMS?

_____
_____
_____
_____
_____
_____

WHERE IN THE WORLD DOES THIS ANIMAL LIVE?

Color the parts of the world where this animal lives.

WHAT OTHER ANIMALS LIVE IN THE SAME REGIONS?

STORY WRITING TIME

Look at the picture and write a story about it.

TITLE:

WATCH A DOCUMENTARY ABOUT SAVANNA ELEPHANTS

Draw a scene from your movie!

What did you learn?

DRAW A PICTURE OF THE ANIMAL

ALL ABOUT BIRDS-OF-PARADISE

WRITE DOWN FOUR FACTS ABOUT THIS KIND OF ANIMAL:

1. _____

2. _____

3. _____

4. _____

RESEARCH & DISCOVERIES
USE LIBRARY BOOKS, ENCYCLOPEDIAS OR THE INTERNET TO LEARN MORE.
BIRDS-OF-PARADISE

WRITE OR DRAW TO SHOW WHAT YOU LEARNED

LEARN & DRAW
BIRDS-OF-PARADISE

Draw My Habitat

Draw My Enemies

Draw My Food

Draw My Babies

WHY IS THIS ANIMAL ENDANGERED?

_____
_____
_____
_____
_____
_____
_____
_____

CREATE AN ILLUSTRATION TO SHOW THE PROBLEMS FACING THIS ANIMAL:

WHAT CAN BE DONE TO SOLVE THESE PROBLEMS?

_____
_____
_____
_____
_____
_____

WHERE IN THE WORLD DOES THIS ANIMAL LIVE?

Color the parts of the world where this animal lives.

WHAT OTHER ANIMALS LIVE IN THE SAME REGIONS?

STORY WRITING TIME

Look at the picture and write a story about it.

TITLE:

_____

_____
_____
_____
_____
_____

WATCH A DOCUMENTARY ABOUT BIRDS-OF-PARADISE

Draw a scene from your movie!

What did you learn?

DRAW A PICTURE OF THE ANIMAL

ALL ABOUT OKAPIS

WRITE DOWN FOUR FACTS ABOUT THIS KIND OF ANIMAL:

1. _____
_____

2. _____
_____

3. _____
_____

4. _____
_____

RESEARCH & DISCOVERIES
USE LIBRARY BOOKS, ENCYCLOPEDIAS OR THE INTERNET TO LEARN MORE.

OKAPIS

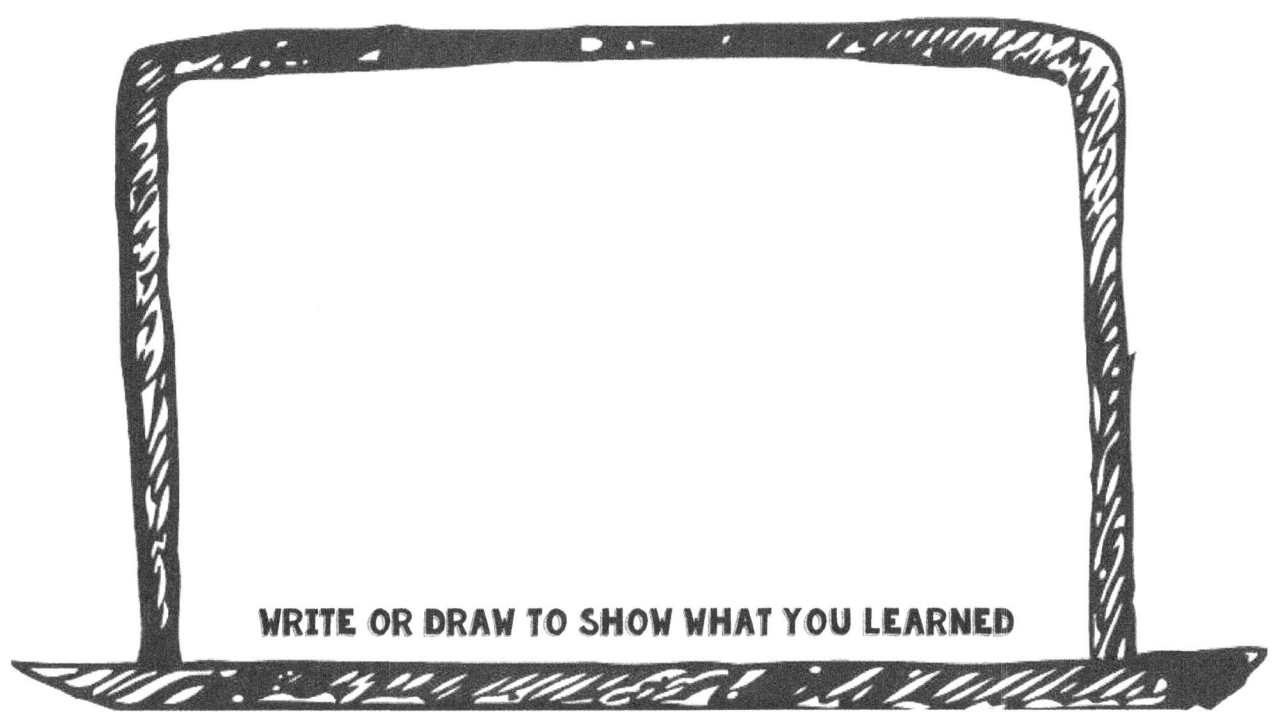

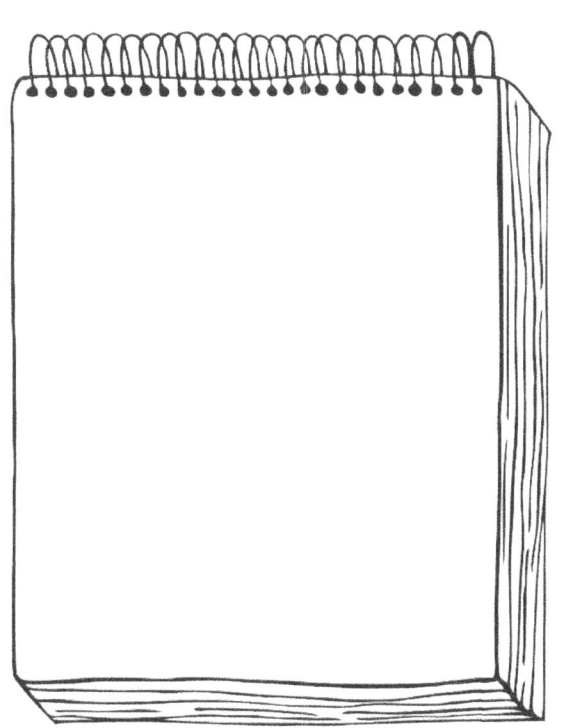

WRITE OR DRAW TO SHOW WHAT YOU LEARNED

LEARN & DRAW
OKAPIS

Draw My Habitat

Draw My Enemies

Draw My Food

Draw My Babies

WHY IS THIS ANIMAL ENDANGERED?

_____
_____
_____
_____
_____
_____
_____
_____
_____

CREATE AN ILLUSTRATION TO SHOW THE PROBLEMS FACING THIS ANIMAL:

WHAT CAN BE DONE TO SOLVE THESE PROBLEMS?

_____
_____
_____
_____
_____
_____

WHERE IN THE WORLD DOES THIS ANIMAL LIVE?

Color the parts of the world where this animal lives.

WHAT OTHER ANIMALS LIVE IN THE SAME REGIONS?

STORY WRITING TIME

Look at the picture and write a story about it.

TITLE:

_____
_____
_____
_____
_____
_____
_____

WATCH A DOCUMENTARY ABOUT OKAPIS

Draw a scene from your movie!

What did you learn?

DRAW A PICTURE OF THE ANIMAL

ALL ABOUT BLUE WHALES

WRITE DOWN FOUR FACTS ABOUT THIS KIND OF ANIMAL:

1. _____

2. _____

3. _____

4. _____

RESEARCH & DISCOVERIES
USE LIBRARY BOOKS, ENCYCLOPEDIAS OR THE INTERNET TO LEARN MORE.
BLUE WHALES

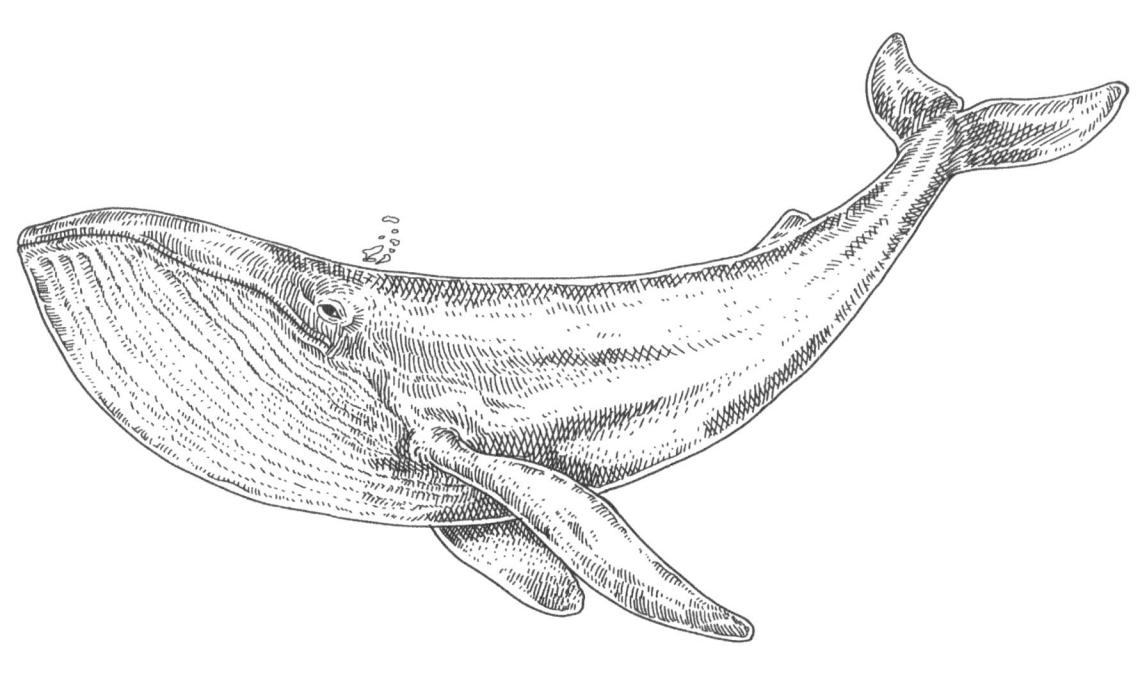

WRITE OR DRAW TO SHOW WHAT YOU LEARNED

LEARN & DRAW
BLUE WHALES

Draw My Habitat

Draw My Enemies

Draw My Food

Draw My Babies

WHY IS THIS ANIMAL ENDANGERED?

_____
_____
_____
_____
_____
_____
_____
_____
_____

CREATE AN ILLUSTRATION TO SHOW THE PROBLEMS FACING THIS ANIMAL:

WHAT CAN BE DONE TO SOLVE THESE PROBLEMS?

_____
_____
_____
_____
_____
_____
_____

WHERE IN THE WORLD DOES THIS ANIMAL LIVE?

Color the parts of the world where this animal lives.

WHAT OTHER ANIMALS LIVE IN THE SAME REGIONS?

STORY WRITING TIME
Look at the picture and write a story about it.

TITLE:

WATCH A DOCUMENTARY ABOUT BLUE WHALES

Draw a scene from your movie!

What did you learn?

DRAW A PICTURE OF THE ANIMAL

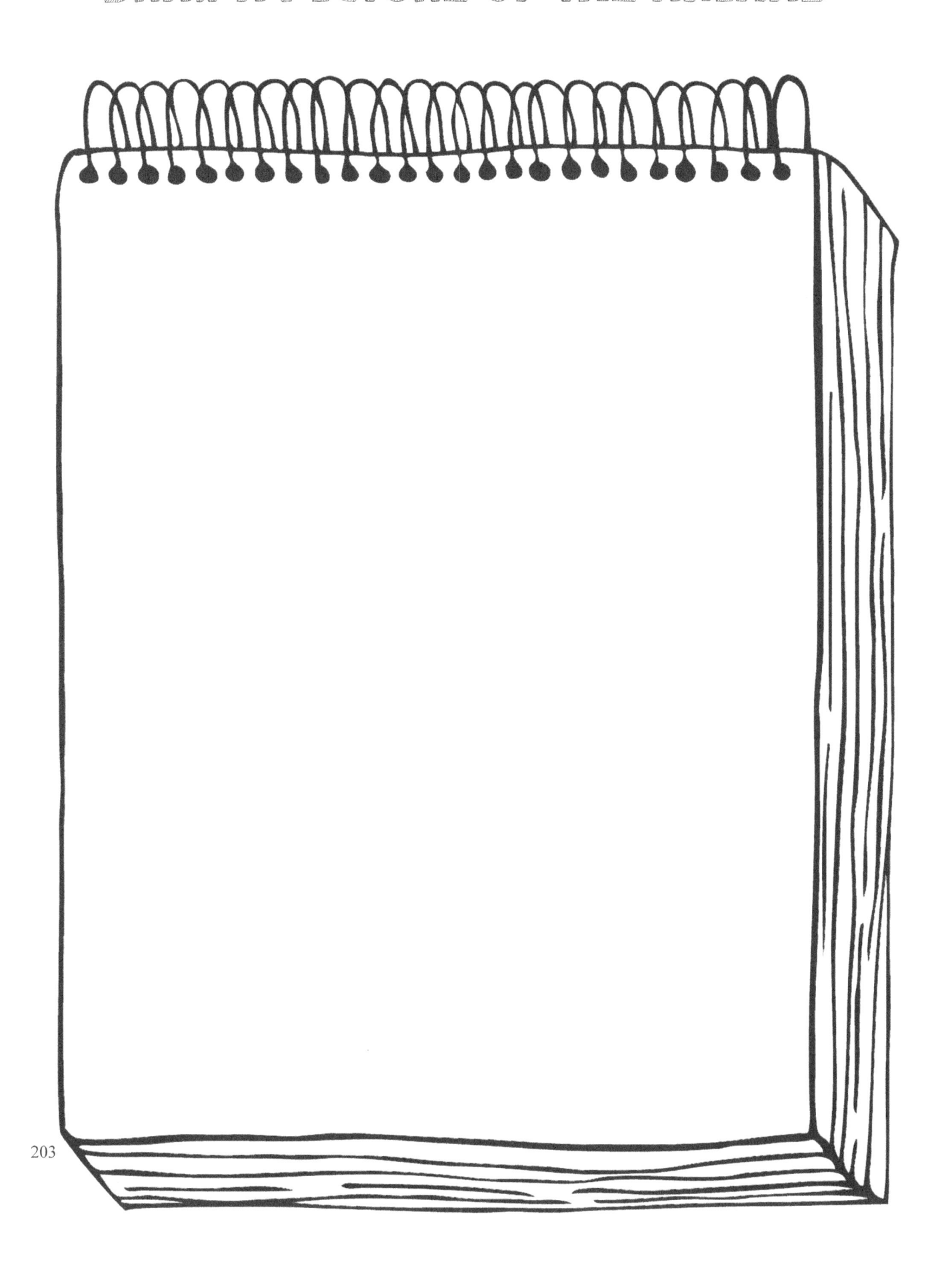

ALL ABOUT IBERIAN LYNXES

WRITE DOWN FOUR FACTS ABOUT THIS KIND OF ANIMAL:

1. _____

2. _____

3. _____

4. _____

RESEARCH & DISCOVERIES
USE LIBRARY BOOKS, ENCYCLOPEDIAS OR THE INTERNET TO LEARN MORE.
IBERIAN LYNXES

WRITE OR DRAW TO SHOW WHAT YOU LEARNED

LEARN & DRAW
IBERIAN LYNXES

Draw My Habitat

Draw My Enemies

Draw My Food

Draw My Babies

WHY IS THIS ANIMAL ENDANGERED?

_____
_____
_____
_____
_____
_____
_____
_____
_____
_____

CREATE AN ILLUSTRATION TO SHOW THE PROBLEMS FACING THIS ANIMAL:

WHAT CAN BE DONE TO SOLVE THESE PROBLEMS?

_____
_____
_____
_____
_____
_____

WHERE IN THE WORLD DOES THIS ANIMAL LIVE?

Color the parts of the world where this animal lives.

WHAT OTHER ANIMALS LIVE IN THE SAME REGIONS?

STORY WRITING TIME

Look at the picture and write a story about it.

TITLE:

_____
_____
_____
_____
_____
_____
_____

WATCH A DOCUMENTARY ABOUT IBERIAN LYNXES

Draw a scene from your movie!

What did you learn?

212

DRAW A PICTURE OF THE ANIMAL

ALL ABOUT PANGOLINS

WRITE DOWN FOUR FACTS ABOUT THIS KIND OF ANIMAL:

1. _____

2. _____

3. _____

4. _____

RESEARCH & DISCOVERIES
USE LIBRARY BOOKS, ENCYCLOPEDIAS OR THE INTERNET TO LEARN MORE.
PANGOLINS

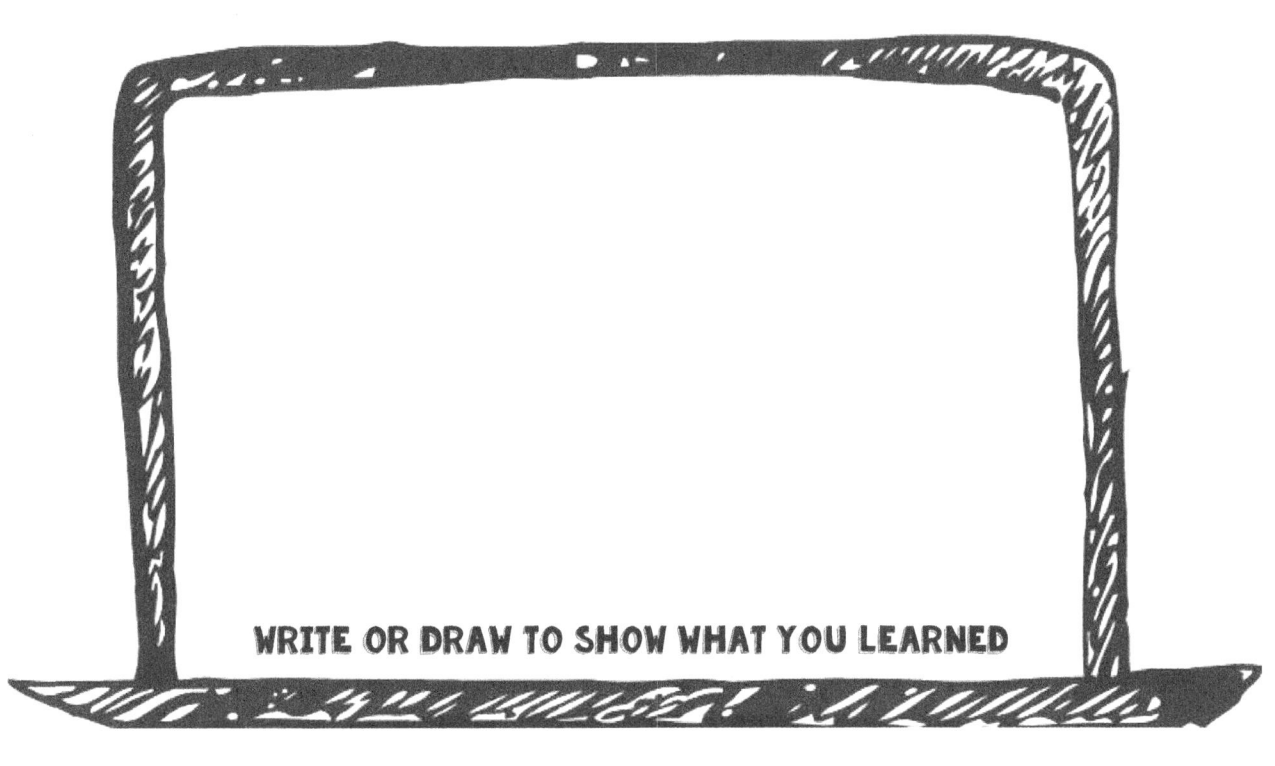

WRITE OR DRAW TO SHOW WHAT YOU LEARNED

LEARN & DRAW
PANGOLINS

Draw My Habitat

Draw My Enemies

Draw My Food

Draw My Babies

WHY IS THIS ANIMAL ENDANGERED?

_____
_____
_____
_____
_____
_____
_____
_____
_____
_____

CREATE AN ILLUSTRATION TO SHOW THE PROBLEMS FACING THIS ANIMAL:

WHAT CAN BE DONE TO SOLVE THESE PROBLEMS?

_____
_____
_____
_____
_____
_____

WHERE IN THE WORLD DOES THIS ANIMAL LIVE?

Color the parts of the world where this animal lives.

WHAT OTHER ANIMALS LIVE IN THE SAME REGIONS?

STORY WRITING TIME

Look at the picture and write a story about it.

TITLE:

___

WATCH A DOCUMENTARY ABOUT PANGOLINS

Draw a scene from your movie!

What did you learn?

DRAW A PICTURE OF THE ANIMAL

ALL ABOUT WESTERN LOWLAND GORILLAS

WRITE DOWN FOUR FACTS ABOUT THIS KIND OF ANIMAL:

1. _____
_____

2. _____
_____

3. _____
_____

4. _____
_____

RESEARCH & DISCOVERIES
USE LIBRARY BOOKS, ENCYCLOPEDIAS OR THE INTERNET TO LEARN MORE.
WESTERN LOWLAND GORILLAS

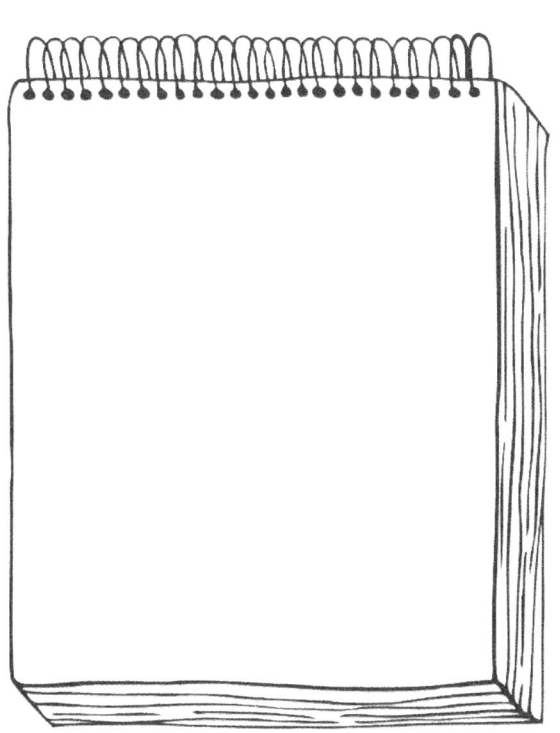

WRITE OR DRAW TO SHOW WHAT YOU LEARNED

LEARN & DRAW
WESTERN LOWLAND GORILLAS

Draw My Habitat

Draw My Enemies

Draw My Food

Draw My Babies

WHY IS THIS ANIMAL ENDANGERED?

_____
_____
_____
_____
_____
_____
_____
_____
_____

CREATE AN ILLUSTRATION TO SHOW THE PROBLEMS FACING THIS ANIMAL:

WHAT CAN BE DONE TO SOLVE THESE PROBLEMS?

_____
_____
_____
_____
_____
_____

WHERE IN THE WORLD DOES THIS ANIMAL LIVE?

Color the parts of the world where this animal lives.

WHAT OTHER ANIMALS LIVE IN THE SAME REGIONS?

STORY WRITING TIME

Look at the picture and write a story about it.

TITLE:

_____

_____
_____
_____
_____
_____

WATCH A DOCUMENTARY ABOUT WESTERN LOWLAND GORILLAS

Draw a scene from your movie!

What did you learn?

DRAW A PICTURE OF THE ANIMAL

ALL ABOUT
BLACK FOOTED FERRETS

WRITE DOWN FOUR FACTS ABOUT THIS KIND OF ANIMAL:

1. _____
   _____

2. _____
   _____

3. _____
   _____

4. _____
   _____

RESEARCH & DISCOVERIES
USE LIBRARY BOOKS, ENCYCLOPEDIAS OR THE INTERNET TO LEARN MORE.
BLACK FOOTED FERRETS

WRITE OR DRAW TO SHOW WHAT YOU LEARNED

LEARN & DRAW
BLACK FOOTED FERRETS

Draw My Habitat

Draw My Enemies

Draw My Food

Draw My Babies

WHY IS THIS ANIMAL ENDANGERED?

CREATE AN ILLUSTRATION TO SHOW THE PROBLEMS FACING THIS ANIMAL:

WHAT CAN BE DONE TO SOLVE THESE PROBLEMS?

WHERE IN THE WORLD DOES THIS ANIMAL LIVE?

Color the parts of the world where this animal lives.

WHAT OTHER ANIMALS LIVE IN THE SAME REGIONS?

STORY WRITING TIME
Look at the picture and write a story about it.

TITLE: _____

_____
_____
_____
_____
_____
_____

WATCH A DOCUMENTARY ABOUT BLACK FOOTED FERRETS

Draw a scene from your movie!

What did you learn?

DRAW A PICTURE OF THE ANIMAL

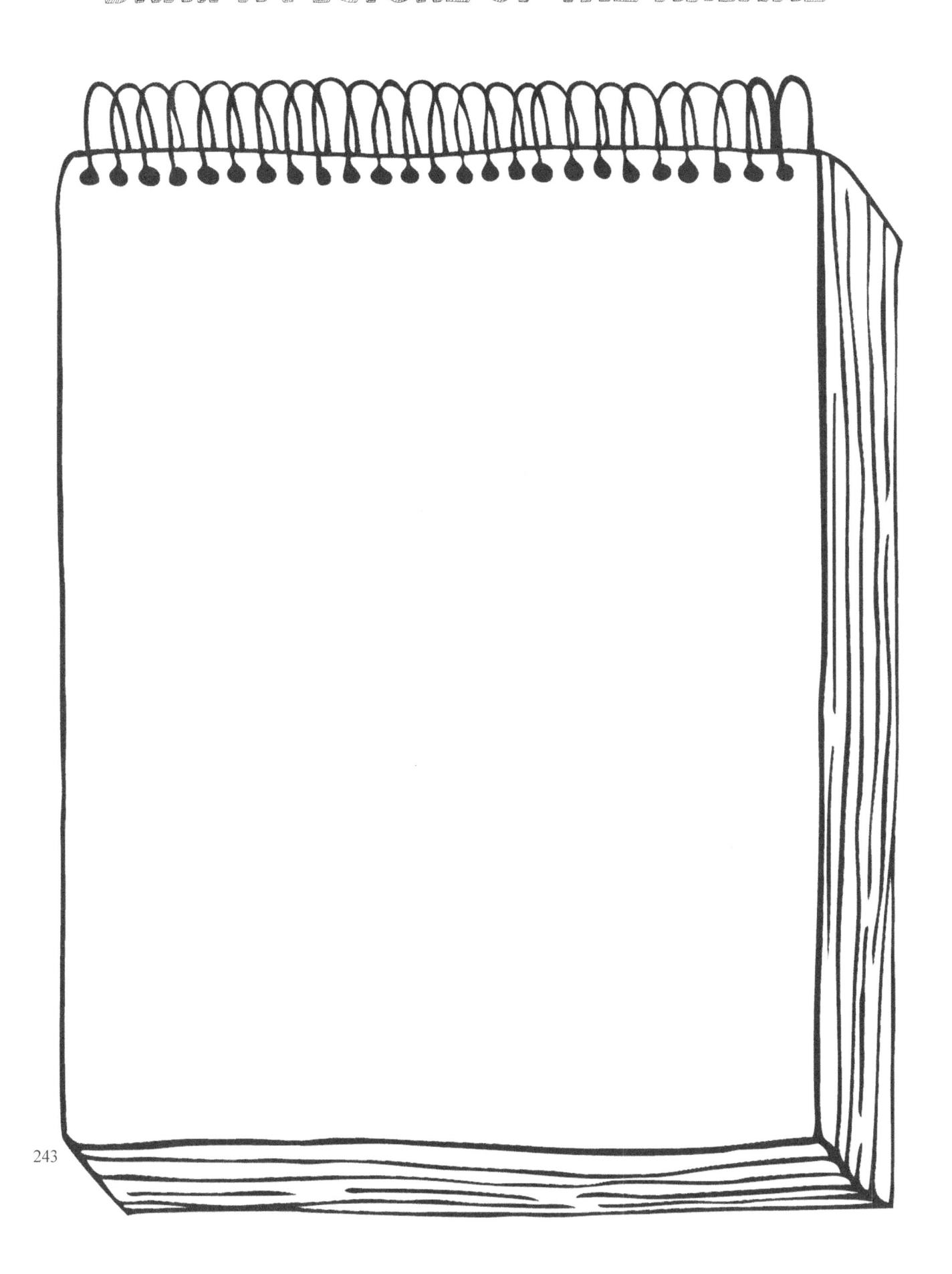

ALL ABOUT
GIANT PANDAS

WRITE DOWN FOUR FACTS ABOUT THIS KIND OF ANIMAL:

1. _____
_____

2. _____
_____

3. _____
_____

4. _____
_____

RESEARCH & DISCOVERIES
USE LIBRARY BOOKS, ENCYCLOPEDIAS OR THE INTERNET TO LEARN MORE.
GIANT PANDAS

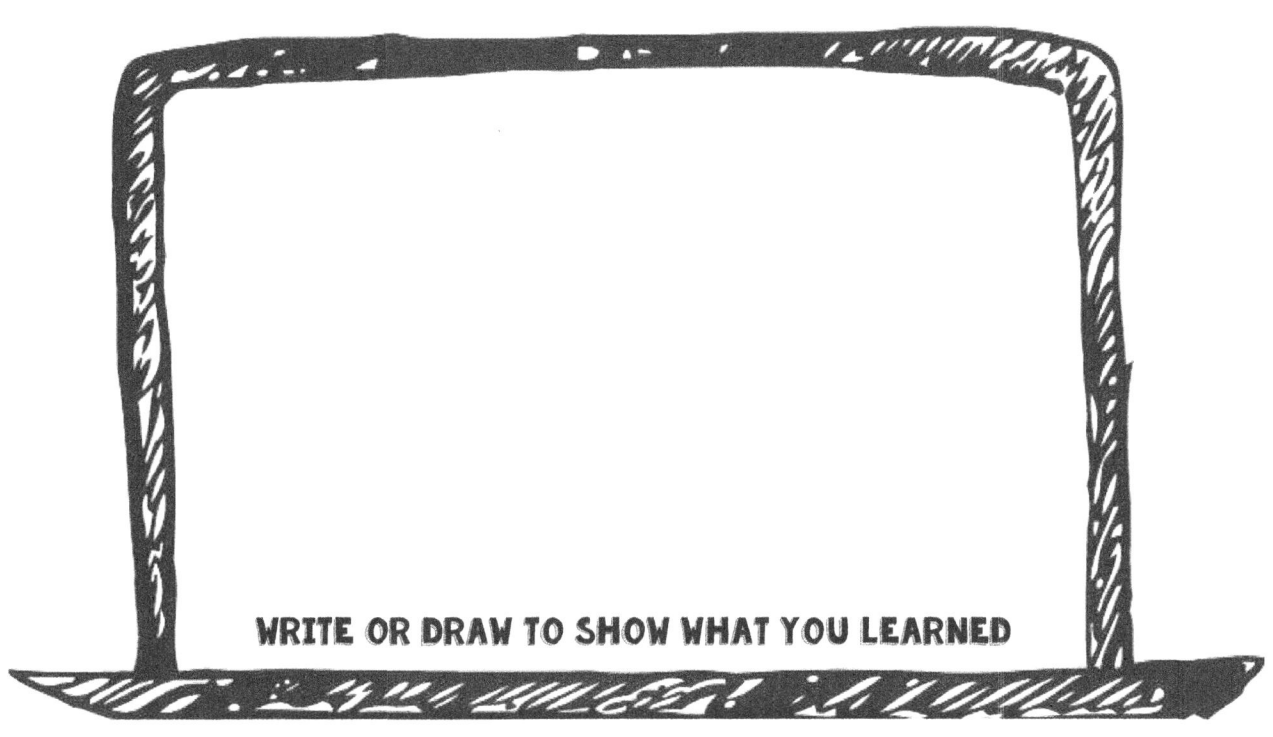

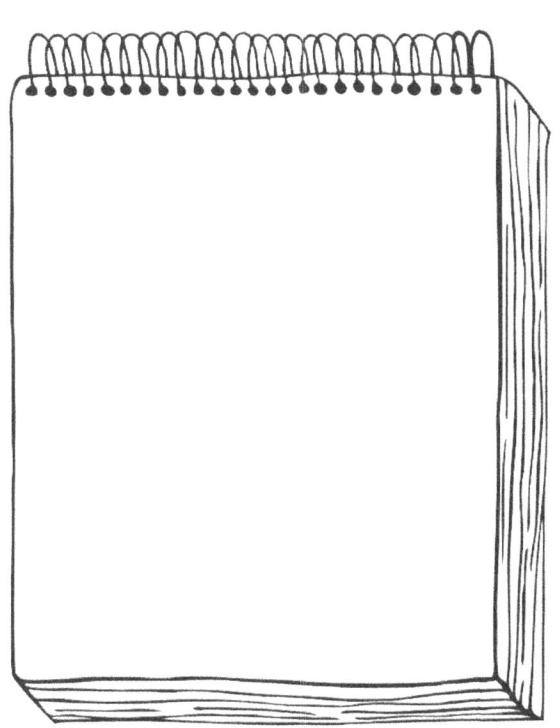

WRITE OR DRAW TO SHOW WHAT YOU LEARNED

LEARN & DRAW
GIANT PANDAS

Draw My Habitat

Draw My Enemies

Draw My Food

Draw My Babies

WHY IS THIS ANIMAL ENDANGERED?

CREATE AN ILLUSTRATION TO SHOW THE PROBLEMS FACING THIS ANIMAL:

WHAT CAN BE DONE TO SOLVE THESE PROBLEMS?

WHERE IN THE WORLD DOES THIS ANIMAL LIVE?

Color the parts of the world where this animal lives.

WHAT OTHER ANIMALS LIVE IN THE SAME REGIONS?

STORY WRITING TIME

Look at the picture and write a story about it.

TITLE:

WATCH A DOCUMENTARY ABOUT
GIANT PANDAS

Draw a scene from your movie!

What did you learn?

DRAW A PICTURE OF THE ANIMAL

ALL ABOUT
AMUR LEOPARDS

WRITE DOWN FOUR FACTS ABOUT THIS KIND OF ANIMAL:

1. _____
   _____
2. _____
   _____
3. _____
   _____
4. _____
   _____

RESEARCH & DISCOVERIES
USE LIBRARY BOOKS, ENCYCLOPEDIAS OR THE INTERNET TO LEARN MORE.
AMUR LEOPARDS

WRITE OR DRAW TO SHOW WHAT YOU LEARNED

LEARN & DRAW
AMUR LEOPARDS

Draw My Habitat

Draw My Enemies

Draw My Food

Draw My Babies

WHY IS THIS ANIMAL ENDANGERED?

CREATE AN ILLUSTRATION TO SHOW THE PROBLEMS FACING THIS ANIMAL:

WHAT CAN BE DONE TO SOLVE THESE PROBLEMS?

WHERE IN THE WORLD DOES THIS ANIMAL LIVE?

Color the parts of the world where this animal lives.

WHAT OTHER ANIMALS LIVE IN THE SAME REGIONS?

STORY WRITING TIME

Look at the picture and write a story about it.

TITLE:

___
___
___
___
___
___
___

WATCH A DOCUMENTARY ABOUT AMUR LEOPARDS

Draw a scene from your movie!

What did you learn?

DRAW A PICTURE OF THE ANIMAL

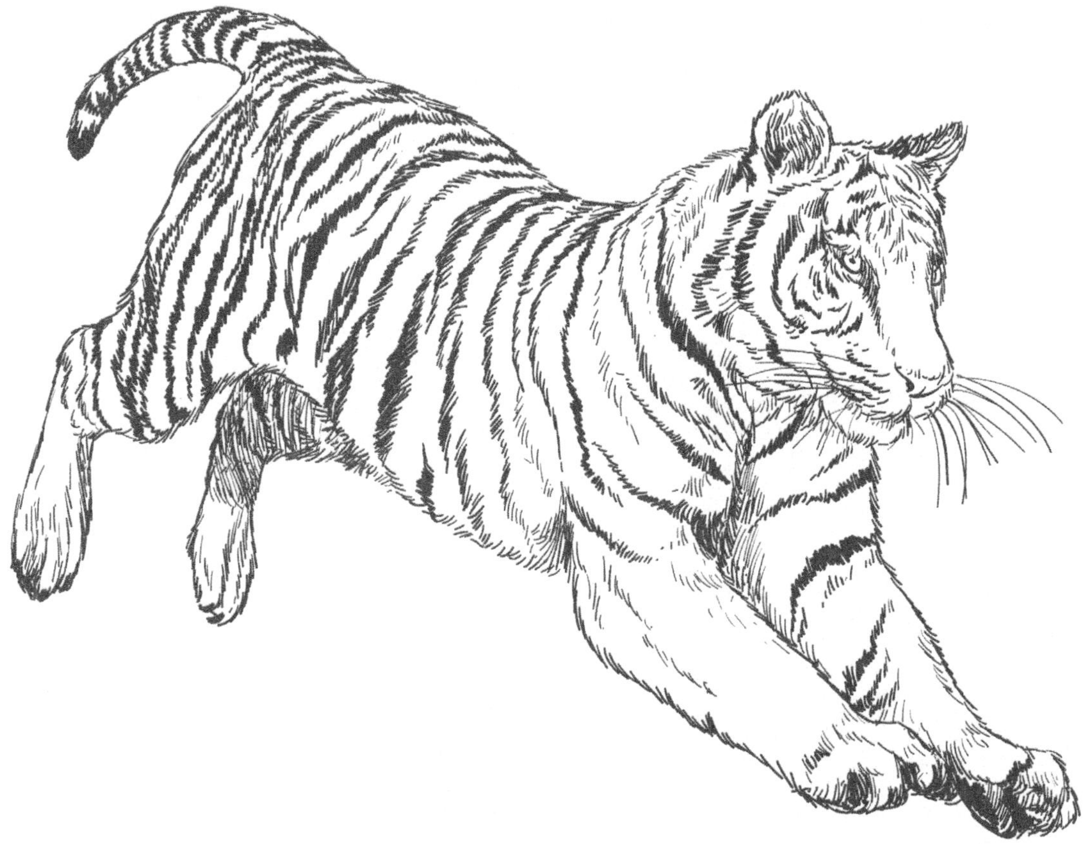

MY ENDANGERED SPECIES DRAWINGS AND NOTES

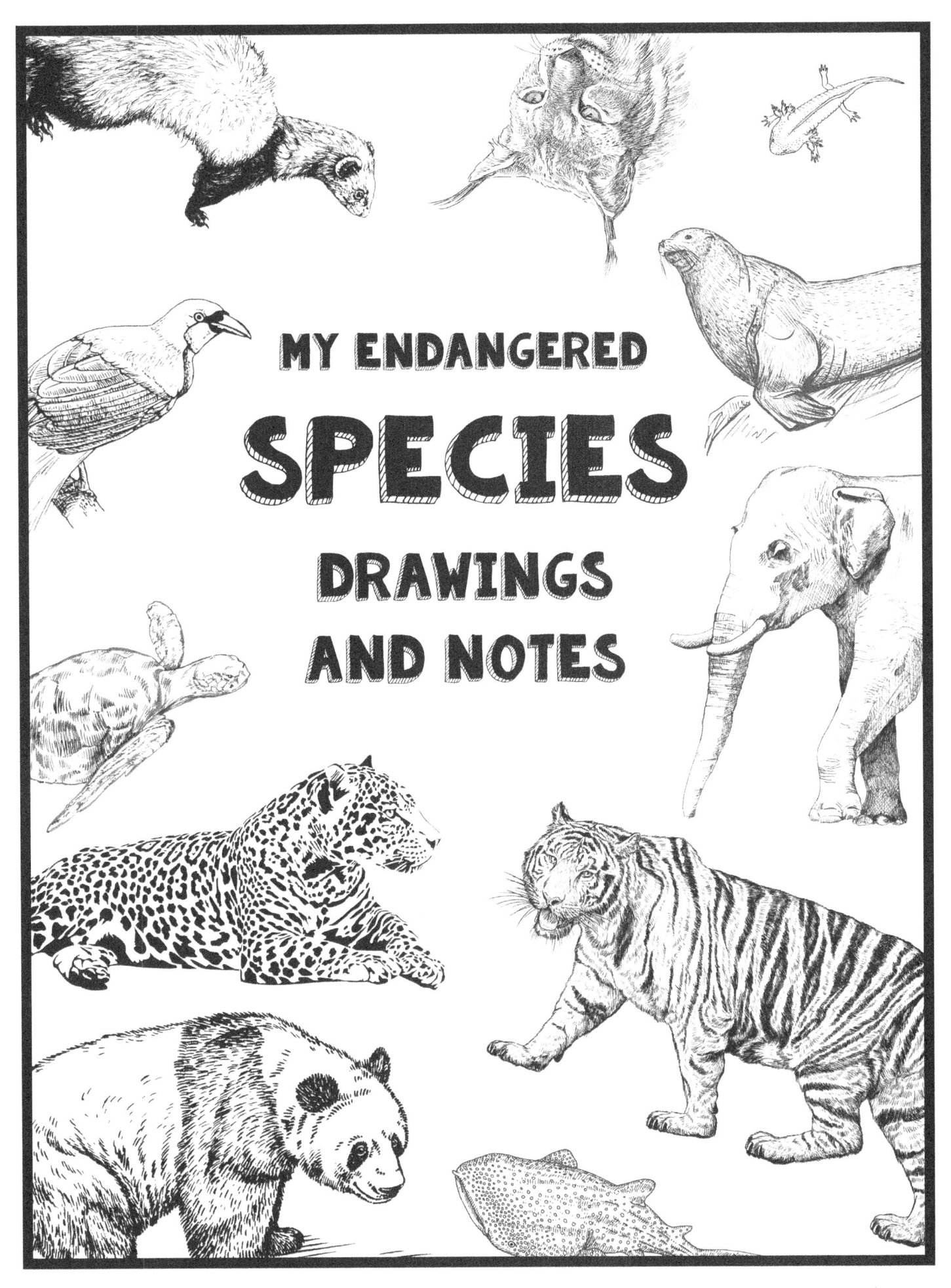

COPYRIGHT 2017
THE THINKING TREE, LLC

FunSchoolingBooks.com

Do Not Copy
All Rights Reserved

Made in the USA
Middletown, DE
10 May 2024